IS SOMETHING *beautiful* IN EVERY DAY

A collection of inspirational writing
from Kim at Sand & Stone Jewelry

KIM LIVINGSTONE

There is Something Beautiful in Every Day
Copyright © 2021 by Kim Livingstone

All rights reserved. No part of this publication may be reproduced, distributed, or transmitted in any form or by any means, including photocopying, recording, or other electronic or mechanical methods, without the prior written permission of the author, except in the case of brief quotations embodied in critical reviews and certain other non-commercial uses permitted by copyright law.

Tellwell Talent
www.tellwell.ca

ISBN
978-0-2288-6371-7 (Hardcover)
978-0-2288-6368-7 (Paperback)
978-0-2288-6369-4 (eBook)

To my kids:

I need you to know, that I will spend every day this life gives me, showing you how much you are loved.

Hoping that my love carries you on your hard days, and without you knowing it, your love carrying me on my hard days.

All the laugh lines, frown lines, smiles and cuddles, you made me a Mama and that is the best gift I could ever have.

This book is for you.

To remind you that you can do anything you want with this one life you have to live and that I will be cheering you on, always.

Love Mom.

Creating my jewelry has become a place for me to write.

I didn't expect that.
I didn't expect to find peace in my own words.
I didn't expect to pour out how I felt out
almost daily to people I don't know.
I always say, if only one person sees what I write and needs it
that day, then I have written what was needed to be heard.

I don't know what I'm going to write until the day I post.
Because I write from my heart, I don't know what it's going to say
before I need to say it.

In my writing, I have gotten to know you.
What you love,
What you wish for,
Who you are.
I've been able to watch your stories unfold, while quietly
sitting back and letting mine be written alongside yours.

So I wanted to just simply say thank you.
For being here. Listening. Finding peace in what I write.
Because in that, I find peace in writing for you.

Love this community

I believe,
In providing high quality pieces at a price range that
makes treating yourself or gift giving affordable.

In kindness & grace.

In love & freedom to be yourself.

In living a more meaningful work life.

In balancing motherhood & bossbabe life.

Knowing there will be days that are harder than others.

Failing & succeeding & recognizing both.

In making an impact.

In showing my kids the power of hard work & giving back.

In community & supporting those who cannot support themselves.

In empathy & recognizing that everyone's story is different & important.

In honest relationships with my tribe & customers.

In giving back.

In loving others & building a brand based
on real life, real stories & heart.

In being grateful for another day.

9yrs ago yesterday, I made a facebook page.
I had been making some things for a few months.

I was 32wks pregnant and had a 2yr old running around like crazy.
"What if no one will buy these. Maybe my friends
and family, but I guess I will just try it."
"What if I put my first bracelet up and no one likes it"
"What if people think I am werid for trying this?
What if they don't get what I am doing?"

What if I didn't?
If I didn't start.
If I didn't work harder than I ever have in my life.
If I didn't put myself out there.
What if I didn't try?

I wouldn't be where I am today.
Still working harder than I ever have, still nervous about
putting myself out there, still that girl 9yrs ago.

Except I have you. We have each other. I have this community of love & hope and friendship between people who don't even know each other.

This is a place to come for inspiration, meaningful gifts & community for so many people, including myself.

What if I didn't start.

It's a thing.
#goldheartarmy.

It's not just a gold heart, it's a mission.

What I've built.
What we together have created.

Now recognized in places I never thought it would be recognized. Women having conversations without knowing each other because they both know the heart.

This little army of love, kindness and compassion. Oh and funny jokes.

A real community of women who can show up as themselves, remember who they are and be inspired to live their best days.

That's an army I want to be a part of.

One of my customers hash tagged it and it stuck. Get used to seeing it.

I wear my gold heart proud.

Knowing that you are wearing yours - it's like a secret group - I see you and know what you stand for, kinda wink and a wave when you're out and about.

Love you guys.
My little Gold Heart Army.

I had no idea how many I could feed when I started my fundraising,
but I kept telling myself, 'even if I can only feed one.'

That one won't be hungry.
That one won't look at the kids beside them
wishing for something to eat.
That one will have hope.
That one might change the world.
If that ONE is given the chance.
I need you to know, I am so thankful for every single purchase.
Because every single purchase helps me make sure I am doing
my part to ease childhood hunger in our community.
Your purchase gives back.

Make a point to:
Give more
Be in the moment
Appreciate everything
See the beauty in everyday

Wear your beautiful things
Use your best dishes
Put on that dress
Wear the shoes you've been saving
Tell someone you love them
Today is all we have

Sometimes you need to search for sea shells
with your kids to understand life again.
Sea shells, they're so simple.
Broken and dirty, but who cares, for some
reason they're like gold coins to kids.
You're crouched down, inspecting barnacles, finding the
smallest crabs under the biggest rocks, and celebrating
in the tiniest victories of treasures found.

Let's live every day like that.
Their wonder reminds me.

That this life is amazing. Even in the smallest tiniest things.
Like the beauty of broken sea shells.

Don't save your words
for the right day.
Today is the right day.
Make sure the people you love,
Know you love them.
Make sure that if you were to leave
This world tomorrow, the last things you said to the people that matter,
are what you want them to remember.

This is your story, these are your chapters.
Some may be short
Some may be long
Some will be happy
Some will be sad
But they're yours
And yours only.
Write them the best you can.
It's your life, and no matter what,
Your chapters are beautiful.

The beautiful parts of you that make you
different from every other person on this planet.

The parts of your story that aren't so beautiful,
but beautiful because they are a part of who you are.

I want you to be brave with your story.
To live for the book that needs to be written, the book about You.

Remember that no matter what,
today you are alive.
You are breathing.
You have the choice to find a piece of joy,
Even if you feel like you can't,
You can.
I promise.

Find one thing that will bring you joy today.
Find one thing that is beautiful today.
Find one thing you can let go of today.
Find one thing you love about yourself today.

Your different is your beautiful.

This is not your practice life.
So GO, and live.
Fill your moments with happy.
Watch the sunrise.
Look for shooting stars.
Whatever living means to you,
just go.

You are good enough,
Smart enough
Beautiful enough
And strong enough
Believe it, it's true.

Like the strongest roots on the tallest trees,
I will grow wide and deep,
I will create a foundation of strength for my life.
I will stretch, grow and break,
but I will never move from who I am.

If you are going to rise, you might as well shine
Get out there - let YOUR light shine, yours – no one else's.

You are what is beautiful and what this world needs.

Do it.
Cross oceans for people.
Give more than they do.
Hold the door open, smile even when they don't.
This life isn't about what you gain,
it's about what you give.

I do enough memorial pieces to know we are
not guaranteed anything, or any day.
I feel like somedays life is going so insanely fast,
that we are going through our days, just to get to the next.
That the years are merging into days.

Let's be done with that.
Go live right now.
Do the things that make you happy.

Let the years take their time.

The things that make me unique are what will propel me
to love what is unique about others – this is how I want to live my life.
That's what is important to me.

To love others like I am learning to love myself.

To all of you:
Mamas
Business owners
Students
Workers
Daughters
Every single one of you.
You are enough.

This is for you.
This is for your life and the way you want to live it.

Go to sleep earlier, drink more water, or whatever you need to make you smile, and bring you back to your foundation.

Whatever it takes to remember your why.

I know there are things about me that I always second guess.
Like sometimes I laugh so loud it's almost like
a cackle and actually turns heads.
So I programmed myself to know when I was going to laugh
too hard so I wouldn't be too loud. Well what the actual!!
Stop myself from laughing too hard because I care what others think?
That my laugh might be too loud?
Only as I've gotten older have I grown into recognizing certain things.
Things that I thought mattered no longer do.
Things that I was changing about myself,
not for myself are no longer going to be changed.

I don't love the sound of my voice or my loud
laugh, but it's me. It's who I am.
I am stopping myself from stopping myself.

So if you're one of the lucky ones who gets to hear my
uncontrollable loud laugh, I hope it allows you to let that part
of you you've been making smaller to come out, and be big.
Just be yourself.
You are needed.
You are loved.
Even in your weirdness

At least once today find your song and play it loud.
Dance in the kitchen.
Dance in the car.
Dance while you're doing laundry.
Sing out loud.
Just let it take over your mind.
It might feel weird at first, but let yourself go.
Free yourself from any thoughts that are holding you back.
It's so freeing, Just do it.

Sometimes I get messages, and my customer says something that changes who I am, or even how I think.
Like this one for example. "A masterpiece of milestones" "To wear it as a symbolic piece of hope and encouragement for dialogue into mental health challenges."

After a mini cry, I sat there and just stopped for a bit.
Your mental health, those around you, it's no joke.
I saw this write up the other day - we go to the doctor if we feel sick. Or we go to chiro if something doesn't feel right. But the second you say something isn't right mentally, I need to talk to someone, we don't do it. Or it becomes Or I'm sure you're fine, you're having a tough
time right now, you'll get over it...
When actually, we should just go. Talk out what we need to talk out, be there for someone who is struggling in a different way than you struggle...no one is the same, but we all can support and love those going through something we can't understand ourselves.

You're never alone.
Don't ever feel guilty for doing what YOU feel is right for you.
If something is off, you do what it takes to get your
heart back to where you feel ok.

You are needed and loved.

Think about all the moments you haven't lived yet.

Isn't it amazing to think of all the smiles you haven't smiled.

The conversations you haven't had.

The lives you haven't changed.

Go. You are here for a reason.

Maybe you're at the top of your mountain
maybe you're at the bottom, just starting the climb.
Maybe you can't figure out how to put one foot
in front of the other to even start
but that's just it…all you have to do is put one foot in front of the other.

Keep going.
In one way or another, you are exactly where you need to be.

I see hearts every day,
but it's on the hard days when I see them in
places I've never seen them before,
and for some reason they remind me that I am on the right path.

Even on my hard days,
because hard days are
where you find a piece of your light and
usually start you towards where you're supposed to be.

Fall in love with being alive.
Because you woke up.
Because your coffee is hot.
Because you have a roof.
Because you will smell the fresh air today
and smile at someone you know.
Because we only get one.

So fall in love with your one life.
Fall in love with yourself.

You are beautiful.
And while you might not see it, we can.
On the days you don't see it, others do.

Because EVERY butterfly is beautiful,
and they can't see their own wings.

Why is it we can see beauty in everyone else
and struggle to see it ourselves?
Let's be softer with ourselves.

*

You are your own perfect sunset, something that is colourful
and changing in your own beautiful way.

Let's try and see not only others for their
full beauty, but ourselves as well.
You are so much more than how you 'think' you look.

Be a light for all to see.

Be who YOU need.
Be who the WORLD needs.
Let your kids shine and be who THEY need to be.
It's simple.

BE true: only you know your heart, be true to it - be true to yourself
BE kind: be kind to yourself, let your kindness fill the world
BE you: be yourself, you are beautiful - the world needs more you
BE love: love yourself, love others, love this life. You only get one.
BE free: to be who you want to be, to let
Go of who you think you should be. To live life your way.

I love airports.
People watching.
Wondering where they're going, what's about to change in their life,
who they're going to see.
Coming home after being away,
you're not the same person as when you left.

The break in reality let's your mind rest,
you learn and see new things and then you come home.
Nothing's changed, everything still smells the same.

You saw, learned, and changed and probably didn't even realize it.
That's the beauty of airports.

Slow down.
Enjoy life.
It's crazy how fast life can change.
Our kids are only young once.
Some opportunities only come once.
You only live ONCE.
I always watch the sunset and rise if I can.
I always go outside, close my eyes and take at least two deep breaths in.
I ALWAYS hold my kids hands.
These simple things can take a busy day and make me remember what's important. The older get the more I understand.
Your time is important.
What you do with it and who you spend it with is
one of the greatest gifts you can give yourself.

So gift wisely.

Beauty is in your heart.
You are so much more than the way you think you look.
Your personality • your love and zest for life • your hands
that hold your kids and cook all the meals • your ability
to love even when you can't love yourself • that's true
beauty, and the most beautiful of all is your heart.

So be yourself today, you are beautiful just like that.

This is your reminder.

*

Do your little bit of good where you are.
Those little bits of good add up and will change part of this world

Just a regular Wednesday

Part 1 of the Tutu Chronicles:

Tutu.
Sparkly shoes.
Sippy cup juice box. For grown-ups.

Take out for dinner because I was done adulting and parenteaching.
It's my new word.

Picked up take out in said tutu, with the sparkly shoes,
in Buttercup, windows down listening to George Strait
and singing like Miranda Lambert. I think.

I've had this dang tutu for years.
Got it for $20 and never wore it.
Today we had a birthday parade for a six year old,
so I decided today was the freakin' day.

I feel like we need to start a movement.
Wear the fancy things you'd never think you'd wear and
rock them doing normal things. You go friend. Do it.

Tutu?
So not me.
So don't care!!!
It was fun and totally freeing to wear it.

Next up. I will do the dang dishes in this tutu.
With my sippy cup.

Mamas:

You are allowed to find out who 'you' are after babies.
We give so much, change our whole life for
those wee souls, and that's ok.
We do what we need to do to raise them the best we can.

But there comes a point where we all sit back and think, geez,
I don't remember me.
Who I was before all of this love, craziness, the sleepless
nights, and socks that don't 'feel' right.
My kiddos are 11 & 9 and I'm finally feeling
like Kim is starting to come back...
But what does it even mean?!
Who are you outside of raising those babies
who will one day change the world.

You are beautiful. You are needed. You are that girl who you used to be,
just different. You need to find her. We all do.

I struggled so with so much guilt, wanting to do things for me, outside
of my kids. But what I've learned is it actually makes me a better mom.

Finding myself, lets me show my kids the
importance of knowing who they are too.

On my birthday, I got a tattoo. Okkk. I actually got three. I got 'bella vita' on my palm, which means beautiful life.

This is my reminder that life is beautiful. Even on the hardest days. With kids. With business. With life. That I struggle everyday with something. My looks. My parenting. My ability to run a company. But I'm here. That every day may not be great but I find something in EVERY day that is beautiful.

The kids signed my birthday card and I stole their writing- the way they both wrote 'love' and got it tattooed on my rib cage. So every day I could remember to be strong for them. That their unconditional love pushes me each day.

I just want to encourage you.

Some days are so hard you feel like you can't get though them. But you can.
I see you. You're not alone. We are all in it together.

Love you all, wherever you are in your life.

Just one person.
Asking anyone, someone to help me change
the lives of kids through donations.
The amount of vulnerability in putting yourself out there, not only hoping you love something I made, but hoping you find it in your heart to make a change in a kids life, and bring me a donation, is a lot.

But I want to put myself out there.
I HAVE to put myself out there.
Otherwise I wouldn't be following what's true in my heart.

So thank you for being another ONE. Because all of us ONEs add up to a huge difference in the lives of kids this summer, or through the food programs you donate too by purchasing anything from me.

I am just one. You are just one.
We are feeding just one.

But that one, will be able to shine their light into this world with a little help from us. That is gift we can continually give.
From the bottom of my heart, thank you for being just one.

Here's to chasing sunsets.
Backing up to the river and putting the tail gate down.
Finding new back roads.
Slow drives with the kids.
Soul saving drives with friends.
Making more memories in an old truck –
I really don't know of much that's better than that.
The memories it made before me.
The memories its making now.
The stories it holds, the miles its seen.
The life of an old truck.

Today is a good day, for a good day.
It really is.
We are all allowed to have 'those days' - but in the bigger picture,
every day we wake up, is a good day.

Let the bad go, shake it off, switch your perspective and move on.
Then go outside and take a deep breath,
and remind yourself how lucky we are to be here.

You get to be here.
That makes it a good day.

♥

"Does this tutu make my axe look big?"

Part two of the Tutu Chronicles:

I got a cord of wood for Mother's Day.
And chopped 3/4 of it by hand.
(There's a row in the back too).
Why? Because I love doing it.

PSA: You can love doing things that aren't
typically on a girls list of to dos.

You can chop wood, stack it, make a fire, and still wear
dresses while hopping out of your jacked up truck.

Be who you want to be.
Stop not doing things because of what someone else might think.
Learn what you need to learn and go do them.

Do the things that are 'heart happy' - for you.
Shine your light. The world needs it!

Please note my legs are the same color as the tutu and
the wood - need to work on that for sure.
Also the bags under my eyes are designer.
Sippy cup and sparkly shoes still going strong.

For all you mamas out there.
It's ok to want something outside of motherhood.
Maybe you want to go back to school, maybe you have a side hustle you want to take to the next step, but feel like you don't have the time for, or can't make the time for.

I get it. It's still even hard for me to do shows as it's not even just the time away during the show, it's the week before - I feel torn between all the things my kids need and the need to work for a deadline.
But. You can.

You can have something for yourself outside of being a mom and not feel guilty about it.
I'm still learning. But it's getting easier.

For myself, I turned a small hobby into a full time job and brand, while raising my kids. There are days it is the one thing that saves my sanity, while other days my kids save me from my job. But for myself, I knew I was meant to do something else while being a mom too.

Every show my kids show up, give me a hug, and see me working.
They see what happens at home, and what the final product is.
Memphis always tells me I'm doing a good
job, and says she's proud of me.

I'm proud to show them they can do or be
whoever they want in this beautiful life.
And so can you

Love where you are…

Harder than it seems isn't it.
Always filling our heads with, 'when these jeans are just a bit looser, or when I get to this point in my life, or when my kids are just a bit older.

I'm the first to admit I struggle with this. I am working on loving myself as I am, today, not when I get to where I think I'm supposed to be.
Loving the days as they come not hoping for what is next.
So this is your reminder.
Love where you are. Right now.
Even if you have a baby on your hip and the other one is crying.
Your jeans aren't perfect but you rock them anyway.
Your job isn't great but your lights are on and there's food on the table…

Where ever it is. Love where you are.
Where you're meant to be is coming.

Owning a company allowed me to truly find out what I was made of.
I've never worked harder or been as disciplined in
anything as I have with being a business owner.

I've learned that nothing will ever go as expected and it's
how you come back from those moments that shifts you
into the next level of yourself and your company.

Knowing that you will have good days but allowing yourself to
appreciate the bad, as that's where growth and change truly happen.

Growing yourself as your company grows is a challenge,
but it's all about perspective.

You need to choose every day to get up, work harder than you thought,
and know that if you truly follow your heart
you will get to where you need to be.

Choosing to make your own path is brave.
Choosing to step outside the box encourages others to do the same.

♥

You just never know what any day will bring.
Yesterday I spoke at a conference, I was full of nerves, sweating through my shirt, and in the middle of all of it, a beautiful lady stood up and shared a part of her story in front of 300 women, about a bracelet she got from me 8yrs ago...

I REALLY need you to understand. You guys EMPOWER me. Knowing you wear my pieces and for years at a time, reminds me on the days I don't want to make anymore, that there isn't another other option but to continue on.

She wasn't going to stand up.
But she did. She didn't know how it would affect me and every other woman in that room. Maybe even someone else who suffers with debilitating anxiety...all of our stories are important and we need to remember that we change others people's lives daily....even in the simplest of actions.

Here's to bracelets that remind you.
Here's to the courage to speak your story.
Here's to always choosing to move forward.
Thanks for letting me share my days with you guys.

How old are your stories?
Simple question. How old are they actually? When was the last time you added to your memories?! Lived a little?!

So this week:
Make a new story. Make a new memory.
Jump in the lake with your kids even though it will be cold, go for a hike and keep your eyes open for something cool. Maybe you'll see Sasquatch.

Let's make our lives the best little story book written.
But most of the time that means we need to get up and go write it.
I challenge you this weekend to write a new story.
Be silly, live a little, go outside of your comfort zone.

Choose living, over existing.
We only get one of these things called life.

To be beautiful means to be yourself.
You don't need to be accepted by others, you need to accept yourself

May you see beauty, all the days of your life.
In unfocused pictures.
In imperfect days.
In messy kitchens.
In your kids dirty faces.
In all things.
Give everything you have to living true.
For yourself.
For your kids.
For your one life.

The you that you are right now.
This you.

Its every bit of beautiful that life has given you.
And every bit of hard that life has thrown at you,
All those moments have made you, you.
Today.
Embrace it.

Ladies.
Roll those windows down!!
Yes your hair will get messy.
Yes you shouldn't put on lip gloss, before rolling down said window.
Who cares!
The freedom that comes with your sunroof open, windows down, fresh air coming in - it's worth looking like a hot mess.

So if you see me, I'll be rocking my own hot mess all summer. It's my therapy.
Also it's the only way not to overheat in the Bronco. But even in my SUV, windows are down always before AC.

It's my rule.
So crank the music.
Be a hot mess.
And feel the freedom.

Wild & free.

♥

"What!! Like you haven't hid in your closet while wearing
a tutu with a chocolate bar and a sippy cup before!?

Part 3 of the Tutu Chronicles:

Listen.
Whatever break you need to take, take it.

Hide in the closet, in the car, in the shower, in the pantry
(this is also convenient because snacky snacks live there)
whatever you need to do, I'm here for it!

It was actually quite cozy in there.
Like I could make a small fort in the shirts and take a nap.

Then of course Atlas the puppy found me -
like why do they always find us!

Animals have some weird sense that triggers when they know we need
a break so they run and find us like the best kind of hide and seek.
Except we don't want to be 'seeked' –
also the same with the small spawn we call children.

Anyhow. Find some chocolate.
A tutu and a closet.
Extra win: sparkly shoes and a sippy cup.

What's your Legacy?
This is your one life, what will you do with it?
Legacy is fundamental to what it is to be human.

Research shows that without a sense of working to create a legacy, adults lose meaning in life.

It gives you a perspective on what's important.
Makes you work for something you get to share with others.
What you get to leave behind.

Your life is important while you are living, and it's important to be able to leave a part of your light behind when your story is over.

What's yours?

Embrace your inner beauty.
I need to read those words.

The one thing no one else has - is my heart.
That one always brings be back to a space I need to be in.

The gifts I've been given, all the things that
make me who I am. It's just me.
Just like no one is you.

How amazing is that.
So take what you have to offer to this world, and go.

Be yourself, arms wide open to everything that makes you, YOU.
This is your high five for today.

Now go, show off that beautiful life that is yours only.

♥

"a ship is always safe at shore, but that is not what it was made for"
- Albert Einstein.

We are made for more than we even feel like we are capable of.
Maybe it's time you let your feet leave the safety
of the shore and jump in that ship.

You can always find your way back.
But if you never leave, you will never know what's out there.

So leave the harbour, like a ship going out to sea.
Feel the unknown, write your story, and
return home when the time is right.

Your ship will be safe at shore time and time again.
And those adventures will live in your heart.

Showing you what you are truly capable of.

'luceat lux vestra'
Latin for 'let your light shine'
It's tattooed on my forearm as my constant reminder.

The sun will rise and set regardless.
What you do with that time is up to you.
Journey wisely.

What we choose to do with the light while it's here is up to us.

Only you get to decide what's true for you.
And no matter what you choose, it's the right choice.

Remember her?
She's still there, inside of you...
Let's go get her!!

Part 4 of the Tutu Chronicles:

Just because we are responsible adults doing all the
adulting all the time, doesn't mean the kids inside of us
can't come out every once in a while and play.
So I put on my dang pink tutu, my bright yellow
gum boots and went puddle jumping.

It's freeing to do the things little kids do because they want to do them.
No one is telling them to go jump in a puddle,
they just do it because it brings them joy.

And joy, my friends comes when you let go of who you
think you should be and let yourself be who you are.

You can be sunshine in human form, for yourself,
those around you and the world.

We all know we need it.
So go find her,
find joy,
live this one beautiful life,
and be sunshine for someone today.
Love Kim.

Still standing strong with my sippy cup in hand.

This girl.
She often looks confident on the outside, like she has her ducks in a row.
But usually no ducks are in a row, she's quite self-conscious and very good at second guessing herself.
But then one day, things started to change.
I felt confident. I felt like myself.

My ability to see the success of my company and what I've done with it, has always been put aside. I don't often allow myself to see my own accomplishments.

I'm truly ready to step into who I am.
Like who I really am and who I want to be and where I want my company to go.

Going out of my comfort zone multiple times a day this Toronto trip, showed me a lot about myself.

We were lead through a visualization, and the girl I saw in three years from now actually made me cry. How I felt, how I carried myself. I saw her and I will be her.
Starting now.

Allow yourself to see yourself. Your true self.
Then figure out how to feel what you see.

It's crazy how a couple days away and a switch in mindset can change you.

- all that is possible, is possible for me
- your individual successes are wealth - it doesn't have to be monetary
- bodies are the least important things about us - but
we have made them the reason we do, or do not.
- we don't allow ourselves to have grace in the journey.
- don't work for recognition - do work worthy of recognition
- if we only show up when we have met the 'pre-requisites'
we have put on our body, we are losing out.
- set yourself goals by quarters - not years.
- the bigger the dream, the louder the saboteurs

♥

Think about everything you are.
Not everything you aren't.
Let's focus on all the amazing things we ARE and
stop thinking of all the things that we aren't.

Because all the things that you ARE, make
you your very own beautiful self.
I know it's so hard some days. I do this every day.
Tell myself what's not great or what I don't love about myself.
I'm trying to switch my mindset.

What I am is what I have to offer, and my imperfect self has lots to offer.

In order for good things to come your way,
you must believe you are worthy of them.

♥

I'm a natural blonde, and have always had a
hard time not wearing mascara.
My 'naked' face isn't easy for me to walk around wearing. I know it's
just mascara, but for me it makes me feel 100% more confident.

So as I'm learning to rock my naked face, I salute those of you who do.
As I'm learning to rock my stretch marks, I salute those of you who do.
Also, for all of you who are learning to love yourselves
for whatever reason it may be, when you do, you give
the confidence to someone else to do the same.

You may never even know the person that sees you and applauds you
silently while sitting in her lawn chair, but I'm telling you right now, you
gave her a touch of 'maybe I can do it too' without even knowing it.

Go out there, with the body you were blessed with, tie your
bathing suit up and remember, you are beautiful, strong
and someone out there is praying for what you have.

Sometimes you need to do your
sock folding in a tutu and sparkly shoes.
Because it's the worst job.
Actually even the tutu doesn't help.

Part 5 of the Tutu Chronicles:

Sock life metaphor:

You're carrying all the socks up the stairs as tight as possible
to gently fold them and put them away, then one straggler
falls out, then another drops, then one day all the socks
just fall to the floor in one big mumble jumble mess.

This is life.
No matter how hard you try to carry it all, you
won't be able to keep it all together.

But after they've fallen, those socks get picked up, one by one and
get put together – except the 75% of ninja socks that go missing.

So let some of the socks fall.
Maybe some of them don't get picked up again.
That's ok. Some aren't meant too.

But just remember, no matter how hard you try, parts of your day/
week/month will end up out of your hands. And that's okay.

Life is meant to be lived, one fallen sock at a time.
Maybe all those missing socks know something we don't.

So today I wore shorts.
May sound weird to some, but I don't love my legs, and I definitely don't like them in shorts. Dresses, always.

But today I put them on and was uncomfortable for a while but then decided not to care.
You know what happened next? We went to the lake, went to the pool, went for an adventure, played Yahtzee, played mini golf...did all the things.

I'm trying. I'm trying to practice what I preach. I tell you guys to 'be free' to be yourselves, to let go of all those hang ups, and truly live for you and your heart...and then I struggle with doing the same.

So here's the start of me teaching myself.

Because I want my kids to have the mom that truly shows them to love themselves - which means I need to do the same for myself.

♥

In life doors will always be closing.
It doesn't mean you sit back and leave it closed.
You get up, open it again and see what's on the other side.
Maybe it will have to be shut again, but maybe it won't.

Usually when one shuts, it's because there is something
better behind the next one. So keep trying.
Don't get discouraged.
You never know where the next door will lead.

Just one change in your perspective is all it takes to see things differently.

And listen, I'm not saying you have to do this with all things, I mean the kids need to clean their rooms after the 17th time of telling them, and some days you just need to Skip the Dishes and get food right to your door. You're allowed those days for sure. I'm a full supporter of just saying no, I can't on the days I don't feel like I can cook or clean...

But start by trying once a week: I get to, instead of I have too. See what happens!

I found myself overwhelmed coming back to work after 2wks off. I was not in the best mindset and I literally said to myself, I GET to go down at work. Orders came in while I was gone, I GET to make beautiful pieces for people to wear. Instead of feeling heavy and overwhelmed about everything I had to do, I let that go and just started to write people back and get to work. It worked for me in the moment I needed it.

Maybe it will work for you too.

Maybe you are still learning to love the version of you right now.
But this version of you, is a you that's going to get you to the person
you will fully love.
It's pretty amazing really.
Your own personal ladder of all the past steps you
needed to take to get you to your true self. Fully loved,
fully acknowledged, by you. No one else.

Keep climbing.

"If you want to give light to others, you have to glow yourself."
This is the most true.
Like the old saying goes, you can't pour from an empty cup.

Don't let the fog,
stop you from shining.

Part 6 of the Tutu Chronicles:

Because it's on the days you want to stay in the dark,
that you need to turn and run towards the light.

My wish for you:

That you find the light in every day.

That you run towards it even when you want
to turn and run the other way.

That when the days are dark, please know what
the light will always show up again.

That you shine so bright you will help others out of the dark.

That no matter what, you know the fog will always lift.

And please remember, some people won't like you because you shine
too bright for them, and sista, you keep running towards your light –
show them the way.

Serious unfiltered photo credit to my daughter Memphis!
I was putting orders out this am, looked up and thought wow, that
sun is showing up through the fog like we need to show up for life.
Then I was like TUTUUU!! Ran inside, told her to put on shoes quick
before the fog lifted and we proceeded to run down the road barefoot

Oh man thank goodness my kids are on board
with me showing them how to shine.

Don't be afraid to love, when so many are choosing hate
It actually takes more to love than to hate.

I guess I'll take the hard road.
Love all the way.

♥

My kids are a part of this company as much as I am. They come down and hang out with me, color beside me, help me stamp, put up with me having to run downstairs for a random rush order, answer the door for you when you stop by.

But running a company, working from home full time and being a full time Mama isn't for the faint of heart. It's hard. It's great some days. But then super challenging on others.

I love that I can stop what I'm doing and be a mom when I need too. Some days I don't love having to stop in the middle of a cuff to be a mom when I need too.

I love that I am in the comfort of my own home. Some days I don't love that the four walls of my home feel like they're closing in on me.

I love that I can go downstairs when I need too, it's the only way I've built this brand. Being able to go down when the kids sleep or are playing etc. Some days I don't love that I can't leave it like most can leave an office. It's always there.

But. I made it. I got through my kids youngest years being able to be at home with them all day, and at 3pm every day with them after school. I remember being at a friend's house before I had kids and she had snacks out for her kids when they got home. I thought, I will do that for my kiddos. I will be there for them after school, and I was.

So here's a shout out to all working moms, all stay at home moms, all the moms doing whatever the heck it takes to get through their day.

I see you.
I feel you.
You got whatever comes your way, work wise, kid wise, home wise, and you're strong enough to handle it.

No one tells you how hard some things will be.

Like finding yourself over and over again as
you go through the stages of life.
But what I've learned is that no one can know you, or what you
feel, like you know yourself, even while you're finding yourself.

And that's ok.
Take your time.

A few weeks ago, Jillian Harris shared my watch on her stories. Which I then shared on mine, because 'hello' I died a bit inside that of all the things she can share, for a second she chose me and something I did.

To some this isn't a big deal. That's ok!
To me, it was a big deal. Like my own personal pat on the back, you're doing something right type thing.

Some days it's hard to be an entrepreneur. Some days it's great. But little things like this are like small building blocks of a foundation you didn't know you ever needed.

But this is what I need you to know. When you send me emails, or when you send me pictures of how much you love my products, or things that remind you of me, it's a bigger deal to me than my mini fan club JH moment.

You are my people. The reason I keep going. Your photos and memories you send me of you wearing what I've done is the biggest compliment I could ever receive.

The people who come back, time after time or who are saving for their first piece...you are not just customers to me, you are a part of this family I never knew I would have, or would need.

So thank you.

Just because I can't grow a straight carrot, doesn't mean I didn't try.

Follow me for more gardening tips!
How to grow the most 2020 carrots you've ever seen.

Part 7 of the Tutu Chronicles:

You're going to try many things in your life.
You're going to plant seeds all over the place.

Some of those seeds will hit the cement and not have a chance to grow.

Some of them will be blown away in the wind and
maybe plant themselves somewhere else.

But then, some of them will grow right where you planted them.

On the top half they look perfect.
Green leaves, tall strong stalks.
But sometimes underneath they're struggling.

The thing is, our intention 'seeds' for our lives are always planted
with full faith that they will grow strong and perfect.

Sometimes this isn't the case.

But those imperfect seeds make us who we are, showing
us that life doesn't have to be perfect to be beautiful.

And guess what?
The best part about seeds is that in most
cases you can replant them again.

Plant away friends.
Then bloom in your own way.
Perfect or not.

Bossbabe. A word I didn't understand.

I was unsure of what to say or how to say it - and really, being shy about what I've done, hiding it behind some other lame words. But as I am on this journey of learning about myself, loving myself, and figuring out who the heck I am, I'm learning to step into WHO I am and who I want to be.

"Hey, I'm Kim. I run a successful company that I built from the ground up. I make custom leather cuffs personalized to your story, and apparel so you can wear something with meaning. I am an entrepreneur who has built a brand on real life stories, and heart."

"I will grow my company as big as I can, changing as many lives as I can along the way. I will struggle and succeed and do it all over again every single day. That's what a boss does. That's what entrepreneurs do."

So maybe you're a Boss that just happens to be a Babe. Maybe you're thinking dang it, I will BE a Boss Babe one day. Maybe you just want to be an owner with no babe requirements.

Whatever it is, own it.
Step into it and don't shy away.

I'm notorious for doing that, and I'm done.
I'm done not being proud of what I've built.
So get ready.
This girl is about to shine, and so can you.

You might just see the tops of flowers in a cardboard box.
I see the beauty that my kids saw on the floor of the nursery.

They loved finding all the broken tops that had fallen
off the flowers. They were like treasure to them.

What if we saw things the way kids do?
What if we saw the discarded flowers as beautiful?
What if we saw the parts of life that aren't typically
beautiful, as perfectly beautiful?
Kids can teach us so much, and they don't even know they're trying.

I hope you find one not so beautiful thing this weekend,
and see it as something beautiful.

Don't forget, there is a last time for everything.

The time your little man wants to cuddle you and ends up falling asleep on your chest, for the first time in years, could be the last time.

The thing is you won't even know it's the last time, until there are no more times, and even then, it will take you a while to realize.

So remember, there are only so many of them and when they are gone you will yearn for one more day of them.

For one last time.

I went to therapy for the first time ever, today.
This wasn't easy for me to say or do.
But we are all in this together.
Which means I'm a friend of yours that will be there
for which ever friend needs to hear this.
My first 'talk it out' appt.
Sometimes you just need a different ear, and a different level of advice.
And that's. OK. It's actually more than ok. It's you saying hey, I'm ready
to let go of what I don't need so I can focus on the parts of me I do.
Which is actually what we do every day.

Break the stigma of counselling. Think of it as making a new friend.
But one with super good listening skills and the schooling to
give you some new information. Because that's what it is.
Someone who is unbiased.
Someone who can take your concerns that are tangled in
your mind, and make sense of what you are thinking.

They were given the gift of listening and teaching.
Go to them, let them give this world the gift they were given.
Starting with you.

Because there's only so many more times they'll sneak into our beds.

Because there's only so many more times you'll hear the little steps coming down the hallway in the middle of the night.

Because there's only so many more times they'll reach for you while they're sleeping to make sure you're still close.

Because there's only so many more times before there's no more times.

Having the kids sneak into bed in the middle of the night is one of those things I'll notice when it's not happening anymore.

Until then, I'll secretly hold onto the hope of waking up to small sleepy feet, as many times as they need to still feel that close.

Just another heart rock write up.

I found this tonight right when I needed it.

You know what I love most about finding them?
It's always unexpected. But needed. - They're always imperfect, but perfect. - Just like us, no two is EVER the same.

Sometimes I'm the only one who recognizes it's a heart shape, because it's never a perfect heart. But that's what I love.
Is that I notice.
I see it.
Maybe it was never meant for anyone else to see or even understand.
Isn't that something amazing?

No one is the same. No one thinks the same. No one sees the same. It's what makes us all beautiful in our own way. It's what makes this world beautiful.

Just like every heart rock you'll ever see.

Beautiful on its own because you recognized it was beautiful.

And that's just beautiful on its own.

How many times can I say beautiful. I don't even care.
Beautiful. Beautiful. Beautiful. Beautiful. There's four more times just for good measure.

Color outside the lines today.

Don't be afraid to try something new.

Learn to laugh at yourself.

Get back up when you fall.

Part 8 of the Tutu Chronicles:

Work boots on.
Tutu on.
Picturesque ride on a Donkey named Dixie for a cute post about something completely unrelated to this post

I didn't expect Dixie to take me for a rip, so I wasn't holding on. It made for some serious belly laughs, and a different outlook on what I was going to say.

We can plan anything we want.
But this year has taught us that nothing goes as planned, each day we don't know what to expect.

But honestly wasn't that actually every day before 2020 too??

As we roll with the punches, let's take life less seriously. Let's laugh at ourselves. Let's do things we didn't think we ever would.

If we learn anything this year, it's that we can't prepare ourselves for what's next.

But we can learn stand back up, get back on the right path (or donkey), and chase after those mini dreams we have for ourselves.

Because we never knew what tomorrow holds,
so judge less,
love each day
and make sure your highlight reel is also full of bloopers.

Want to see something inspiring?

Slow down.

Slow down, notice, even on your busiest days,
you can find beautiful things.

Slow down.

Walk by the mirror. There, that's one thing that's beautiful.

"You're beautiful because you know your own darkness and still that alone doesn't stop you from finding your own light." RM Drake.

Stopped to take a picture of a black cloud, so hopeful for a storm and the sun broke through right as I was taking the picture.

I just really felt this today and felt like someone else would too.

No matter where you are, there is ALWAYS light. Remember that.

You were given your body.
You were given your mind.
You were given your heart.
Your eyes.
Your smile.

Those things were given to YOU only.

I admire beautiful people. I love that we all have different shaped eyes, bodies, and faces. It's amazing if you really 'see' it.

In today's social media based world, it's hard to
not get caught up in others worlds.
I'm guilty of this for sure.

So just remember. Someone saw you today and
thought you were beautiful and didn't say it.

'Her' can be her own kind of beautiful, and 'You' get to be yours.
So go out there and show yourself. The world needs a YOU.

The world has an amazing way of showing us that
life has a way of taking care of itself.
The sun will always rise, and the moon will always follow.

Do what you can, and try not to worry about what you can't control.
I know it's easier said than done, but just start with the little things.
Let them go.
Free up the space for the important parts of your life.

It's a game changer.

*

This is the beginning of finding yourself.
Welcome home.
Whatever that means for you.
Welcome back.

What you see:

Me leisurely going for a picturesque ride on a donkey named Dixie in the middle of a field on a perfect fall afternoon.

What you didn't see (Chronicles #8)

Me on said donkey named Dixie grasping at air as I bailed off because she ran from underneath me.

I could've just posted this picture yesterday. But I wanted to show you what happened before this cute pic was taken. Because that's important too.
The imperfections

Part 9 of the Tutu Chronicles:

You only see the highlight reels in others' lives.
Because that's all they show you.

Yes he crossed the finish line at the marathon, but you didn't see the early morning runs and the times he couldn't take one more step while training.

Yes she is on the beach in Maui but you didn't see the extra hours and shifts put in so she could save enough for her dream vacation.

Yes she looks perfect in that outfit but she took 35 pics in 10 different poses to get that shot and she still doesn't feel like it's good enough.

The point is, you see the highlights, the best pictures, moments etc.

And we have to remember that we have no idea what it takes anyone to get to that picture or highlight or get to that dream for their life. Long hours, products that didn't work, tests that were failed, workouts that didn't happen, confidence that appears to be there that isn't.

In order to be successful in whatever you want
to do, you will fail. You will fall.
You will want to quit.

So did the person you look up too.
Or the girl you're comparing yourself too.

This is your reminder to keep going.
Work hard, study harder - get to that picture you have in your head.

Along the way, stop comparing.
Your highlight reel is someone else's dream too.

Went for a walk last night.
Saw a little daisy.
All by itself.
Imperfectly beautiful.
Pieces of it had been lost, but it was still
standing, showing how pretty it was.

Right beside it was a thistle.
It's bigger than the flower, more abrasive looking, and has
a much stronger foundation then the wee little daisy.
Most likely could handle a wind storm or even someone's misplaced step.
Not the daisy, it's smaller and more likely to be
blown over or squished when stepped on.

Yet the daisy still stands.
It still says, I'm here and I'm not going anywhere.
I've lost parts of myself, and will continue my search
for the sun and growth no matter what.
Even when something bigger is in front of her, she still stands.

Let's all be like the daisy.

Say it to yourself if you need it tonight.

I've made it through another day.
I'm going at my OWN pace.
I'm trying my best.
I need to be patient with myself.
One day at a time.

Be patient with whatever you are going through.

Everyday there will be something new. Some part of 'the process' that isn't great or what you wanted. Even when 'the process' is exactly what you wanted, patience and grace is always needed.

The last couple months have shown me many different 'processes.' Some I for sure did not want to go through, some I'm right in the middle of - all which will pass.

Emotionally, physically, financially.

The thing is, is that I still am trying. I'm still waking up every day and finding things I love even when I'm not loving the day.
Some days are happy.
Some days are meh.
Some days are just 'what the actual crap is going on'

I am learning patience with myself.
I am learning to have more grace with myself.
But I am learning that 'part of the process' only gives me a stronger foundation to stand on.

Remember who you are.

That person you are down to your core.
The one who you know you are, find her again.

Remember your why.

Remember what you love.

Remember who you used to be before life
showed you something different.

There is always room for you.
Yes there is.
There is a spot that was made just for you.

So please never feel like it's too crowded.
Your little chunk of this world is just that, YOURS.

So make it comfy and shine away.

Does this fish match my tutu?

Part 10 of the Tutu Chronicles:

Remember last post when I said to go find a piece of joy this weekend?

Well I don't tell you to do things and then not do them myself.

Normally, this is not my fishing attire, but dang rights I put on my tutu, went to the river and caught this fish!!

I love fishing.
I love being outside.
I love rivers.
These things bring me joy.

So I doubled down on the joy finding and was the only one in a tutu standing at the river, because why the heck not.

Because I want to do fun things with my life.

Because in that, I want to encourage you do be silly, be yourself and do what makes your heart happy.

Because I want to do things I didn't think I would.
That's what colouring outside the lines is about.

So again, like all the other tutu chronicles - don't be afraid to have fun and do things maybe no one else would.

Now for the rest of ever I have to wear this fishing because it's my lucky charm.

You started with a blank canvas – now you are a work of art.
Imagine what the next years will bring.
More laugh lines, frown lines - life lines.
All of these beautiful things make you who you are
whether you chose them or not.

And the best part?
No one else will ever have your canvas.

Come alive in all that is subtle and all that is grand.

Do the big things.
Do the small things.
Do the mundane things.

And know that doing all those small or big
things means you are alive and capable.

You just need to see it.

Kids.

We love them with everything.
They test us on everything.

We teach them the best we can every day.
They teach us everything, every day.

Some days we can't make it another second.
Some days we can't wait for another second.

No matter what, they love us with everything they have.
Our hardest days, our best days, they days we
don't think we can do another day.

Get good at saying no to the things that don't get your yes.
This one is SO true. SO hard to learn but gosh you guys,
I used to say yes to everything. ALL the things and I
was crumbling under all the things I said yes to.

Now I ask myself, does this help me get to where I'm going?
Will this cause me more grief than relief?
Why am I saying yes when I know I need to say no to this??

And THEN be strong enough to say no.
Recognize you need to say it, then find the courage to actually say it.
I'm still learning but I'm telling you, nothing
I have said no too, have I regretted.

You'll know it's not right. So stop saying yes when you
don't mean it, and say HECK YES when you do. •

Run towards the right YES.

♥

Two moms.
Two dreams.
Two entrepreneurs.
Two successful companies.
And guess what?

We feel like we fail daily.
Which we do.
We have serious mom guilt.
We struggle with running our companies.
We question whether we can get through another day sometimes.
Business and motherhood wise.

Even though they look successful, some months aren't and
we have our days of okay, we might not make it.
This risk might not work.
These bills might not get paid.
What are we even doing?!
Can we even get through another month?

But we have both agreed that quitting isn't even an option.
Even on our worst days, actually throwing in
the towel just WILL not happen.
Like we will cling on until we can't anymore. We aren't built to quit. •

Because we are moms.
Because we have dreams.
Because we are entrepreneurs.
Because we have and will continue to have successful companies.
Because we have kids looking up to us every single day.

Because it's WHO we are.

So go. Succeed. And be proud of yourself, which include your failures.
They make you who you are.

I don't know if I'll ever be able to put this weekend into words.
Charleston has been amazing.

There were business breakthroughs which was expected and hoped for.
But what I didn't expect was the personal breakthroughs.
I mean really working through some things I didn't
even know I needed to work through.
Both crying and laughing my way to a different me.

Then today. The ocean. You know what it means to
me. I feel like I know myself when I'm around it like it
knows who I truly am. It has a huge effect on me.

We've been talking about the quote that I have on a wrap
- a ship is safe at shore, but that's not what it's meant
for. That there will ALWAYS be rough waters.
The waves will get big and life will always feel like there
are days you can't get yourself above the waves.
But you will.
So be brave enough to leave the shore and get on
that boat to who you are put here to be.
Like me coming all the way across the country out
of my comfort zone to invest in myself.
I left the shore...

Silly boys. Trucks are for girls.

Part 11 of the Tutu Chronicles:

Since Buttercup the Bronco is my truck, I need
to know how to do all the things.
I WANT to know as much as I can about her
and how I can fix her if needed.

So when her boots needed to be put back on after her
motor was fixed, clearly I was the gal for the job.

Ok I never usually wear a tutu when working on Buttercup.
Clearly only when I drive her.

Listen.
You can do anything you want.

You can fix trucks if that's your thing.
You can climb the corporate ladder if that's your thing.
You can be sweet as pie and listen to hardcore rap to calm down.

You can be all the contradictions - it doesn't frickin' matter.
As long as you are living in a way that makes your Heart Happy –
you go ahead and do you.

Because the world needs more you.
Contradictions and all.
Tutus included.

Today is Women's Entrepreneurship Day.
Well I am a woman! And I am an entrepreneur!!

I made something from nothing.
I built this from the ground up.
It's been 9yrs.
It takes time.
It takes consistency.
It takes more love and grace and grit than you can ever imagine.
It takes failing. Daily.
It takes confidence even when you feel the least confident in yourself.
I have had some great success.
I have had some huge fails.
I've had days I wanted to yell from the mountain top
and days where I didn't want to get out of bed.
But I show up. Every. Single. Day.
Because I am an entrepreneur. It's in my blood. And I refuse to give up.

Your heart needs to be the backbone of your company.
Your why has to be greater than making money.
Your why, will get you your how.
Your how will allow you to find your dream.

Stop apologizing. It will make life easier when you are just yourself
I still do this.
Apologize for things I do. For real. I'm awkward, and I
have a loud cackle laugh when it randomly comes out
and I always cover my mouth when it does it usually is
at inappropriate times. Like in a quiet restaurant.

But these things make me who I am.
And I'm ready to live who I am unapologetically.
So let's do it together.

Go out that front door today, your silly, cute self and let the world
know you're here to stay in all your weird and awkward ways.

When it came to choosing a word for the year after
going back and forth 1,000 times, 'love.' was it.

I wanted you to end this year and start a whole
new decade with a strong foundation.

I wanted to give you a solid reminder of who
you are, who you want to be.
To show yourself and the community you live in, that love is
always stronger, always brighter and can change a life.

We can love better.
We can love more.
We can love today.
We will love ourselves.
We do love each other.
We can find love in the not so good days.
We can LOVE. Period.

I WILL be a brand that makes sure everything good is going out into this world, and whatever I make I want you to feel the same wearing it. Like a mini warrior shield of kindness, love and hope.

Have a good day today.
Find a piece of love somewhere, somehow and I
promise it will turn your day around.

Today's my birthday and I have a birthday wish to myself - and for you.

A quick story:
We were in South Carolina for the Rise Conference, it was 22 degrees and I wore a tank top which sounds normal but it's not really my favorite thing to do.

Got to the ocean and we were taking pics and I was constantly trying to cover my boobs for each picture. Pulling and yanking on my shirt and getting annoyed that I couldn't get a picture with them not there.

We made a rule that we were going to close our eyes and just sit on the pier for five mins doing nothing but listening to the ocean. Except in that time all I heard was 'this is who you are' 'this is what you've been given, stand strong, stop finding ways to hide' 'this is who you are'

It was such an aha moment for me.
This is who I am.
This is what I was given.
I have always been uncomfortable in my own body, never really allowing myself to just be confident in this body that does everything for me.

We didn't really look at the pictures until we got back to the hotel and when I saw it for the first time I was like, I see myself. Like actually see myself. I didn't try and pull up my tank top, or cover up, I just let myself be in this picture.

I am so grateful for a hundred tiny things every day. Even for what my body can do for me, I am strong and healthy. But I've always had a hard time being grateful for other parts of my body I struggle with.

So my birthday wish to myself is to feel as free as I felt in this picture that day by the ocean. That I will love my body because it is me and who I am.

And my second birthday wish is that if this is also you, that you remember this is WHO YOU ARE and that you will have confidence to stand in that truth this year and live freely.

So much love to you today.
Thanks for coming on this journey of figuring it all out.

Where the hell would a small town girl climb up?
If it wasn't for trucks.

'If it wasn't for trucks – by Riley Duckman.

Part 12 of the Tutu Chronicles:

Find yourself.
Whatever that means.
I find myself in country music.
The words, stories and lyrics have always resonated with me.
I find myself in my bronco.
It's the one thing I do for me. The one thing that allows me to let go of everything while I'm driving her. I am 100% myself when I am in her.

Put them together and it's the perfect combo.
I find myself as I get older too. More confidence.
Less give a shit.

So listen to yourself.
Do the things that allow you to find yourself.
Make the time for them.

Because in them, you will find all these little pieces of yourself that will build you up to the person you are.

And that's important.
This part of the song - my dad was a fencer...
hit me right in the heart strings...

How would anybodies daddy get around?
To mend the fences and feed the cows

Where would old dogs ride?
Where would life fly by?

I wouldn't be who I am today
If it wasn't for a short bed Chevrolet
(Well Ford - but every song can't be perfect ;)
Then start this week by finding a small piece of you again.

Not everyone will understand why you work so hard.
Work hard anyway.
You just do your thing,
Keep going towards that goal that no one understands.

Maybe you're starting a new class, or at a new gym, or
that new company you can't get out of your head.

Do it for you.

I could've stopped 100x based on other people's opinions.
But I learned long ago they will never understand my heart
and what it longs for. Only I know what is true for me.

So go out there.
Be great anyway.
I'm right here with you.

Be you. Someone might need who you are hiding
This is so true.

We are all here for a reason.
The world and the people need who you are deep down. The real you.

The person you meet is the person I am. This is something
I have never hidden or changed. This is what you get.

So shine bright ladies.
Don't hide YOUR bright.
We need you!

Years can be amazing.
And hard.
And crazy.
And happy.
And sad.
And soul breaking.
And beautiful.

I WILL always pat myself on the back.
From pulling myself up when I felt like I couldn't continue on and then allowing myself to celebrate the beautiful days and things that happened.

So pat yourself on the back too.
Those tears you cried, the laughs you had. They made you who you are right now.

And that makes you beautiful

♥

This Christmas season, my heart turns gratefully to
those who have made my little company grow.

That means you.
Supporting small businesses like mine, means you are supporting
things like soccer, art classes and providing food for my family. I am so
thankful for every single order, which means I am thankful for you.

This season may you find time to enjoy life's simple
blessings and the beauty of each quiet moment. For it's
in the small things that we realize the big things.

My hope for the year ahead, is that you find yourself
living your life fully, whatever that means for you.

Get back to the basics of living and truly
enjoying the life we have been given.

Thank you for your support, we are forever grateful.

Gotta go, I have someone I have to be
Heck yes I do!
And you do too.

Starting each month with a Heck Yes attitude.
I am happy with who I am now,
but I know there is more of me to find...

I've got someone I have to be and I'm going to find her.

Life, I'm coming for you.

Who else is ready to find a part of you, you knew was
in there but had yet to meet. I know I am!

When you rest,
Remember that you are not wasting a day.

Part 13 of the Tutu Chronicles:

Rest and self-care are just as important as the hustle.

Those less busy days add purpose, creativity, energy and extra love into all the things you will do the next day.

It's so common for us to push ourselves, always moving to the next thing on our never ending list.

So make sure rest is on that list.
You can't serve from an empty cup.
And your heart can't change the world with a tired soul.

Even in a tutu.

I'm forever looking at the skies.
Morning and night.
Every day.

Northern BC has the most magical skies.
Sunrises, sunsets, northern lights, storms - I love a good storm.

Some days when it's a harder day or things aren't going
right, besides for seeing hearts everywhere, skies can
bring me right back to where I need to be.

There is such power in that.
To be grounded from looking up.

To be grounded,
from looking up.

Somewhere there is a past you overflowing with pride looking at how far you've come.

Even if it's just one foot in front of another -take one more step. Even if you feel you didn't do all the things you had planned today, or conquered all the goals you had set, that's OKAY.

You're here.
You kept your kids fed,
you showed up for work,
you were kind to someone else,
you saw the sunrise,
you made a super good cup of coffee,
you picked yourself up when you didn't think you could,
you kept going.

Your accomplishments don't have to be huge. It's actually the small things you do daily, that add up to make you who you are.

The you that sat here on this day a year ago, is proud. So make the girl who will be sitting here this time next year, just as proud.

We can get so caught up in all the busy.
We can get so caught up in what went wrong
or who we didn't make happy.
And we can always lose sight of one important thing. Ourselves.

I had stumbled across a picture of myself by the ocean, feeling so
much like who I am deep down. I remember feeling so free.
Reminding myself why I started this company and why I keep going.

Why I made my own lane.

And my why is greater than my can't.

Just know you are stronger than your cant's,
you are stronger than those who say you can't.

Because the lane you're making is yours and yours alone.

It's your road, no one else's.
You get to choose every day which way to go.
You get to choose every day when to stop.
You get to choose every day when to hit the gas.
You get to choose every day when to take a U-turn.

No backseat drivers.
This is your road.
This is your life

Listen.

If you're done sitting around and waiting, then stop waiting.

Go and build it yourself.
You have it in you, so take that fire and go after it!

Your dream.
Your build.
Your success.
Your terms.

When you can't run away from the magic of Christmas.
Or dance to the music of Christmas either.

Part 14 of the Tutu Chronicles

When your friend tells you to repeat a fancy tik tok but your
dance moves are that of a solid wood board, you improvise!

Just because someone is a better dancer, doesn't mean you can't dance.

You just move to the beat of your own drum.
It might not be perfect. But it's you.

And if you're having fun, and it makes you happy, you do it.
Even if you look silly and like you've never danced before.

So do what makes your heart happy.
Wear the elf slippers.
Put on the tutu.
Crank the Christmas music.

Faye this is dedicated to you on your birthday.

Don't send me videos of people who can actually dance ever again.

Kids are so free in expressing themselves in so many ways.
Maybe we should take note and actually live
our lives the way they live theirs.

We should all find that part of us we've set aside as adults.

Full of colours.
Full of hope.
Full of love.
Full of non-judgement.
They just live.
It's time we did too.

Love simple today.

The girl who is going to do big things cannot let small things get to her
Whether this is in business or your personal life, remember it.

On the business side, you will always encounter the 'small things'
except they are going to feel huge. Massive at times. Insurmountable.

Suppliers gone wrong, financial loss, people calling
you down even when you're doing your absolute best,
mistakes, hard days, no balance of life at all days.
All. The. Things.

But you weren't given this calling to let these
things determine your path forward.

Sure you can have some bad moments, bad days and that's allowed.
But don't stay there.

You are meant to do big things, so allow these other things
to come, then push them aside and keep going.

You. Can. Do. It.
You have it in you.
Just choose the big things over the little, and make those hard things
foundation stepping blocks into getting where you need to go.

I'll be right here cheering you on.
Extra Love.

I want a full and interesting life. I only get this
ONE and want to do big things.
That means taking chances, risks, going outside of my comfort zone.

The things that have been sitting on my heart, they're coming to life –
and I want to encourage you to do the same.

And some of these things may not work like I have dreamed them too, but that's ok, there's always another one waiting to come to life - I will ALWAYS keep trying. If you try and it doesn't work out, that clears your heart for the dream that is meant to be.

Maybe this week, get confident enough, brave enough, to do one thing that gets you closer to something you've been wanting to do.
If you do, I will too.
Be brave with your life.
You're loved.

One day, this will be twenty years ago.

Because time isn't slowing down.
Because these moments today, tomorrow and
the next day will be different soon.
Ok different, but different.

So cherish the baby snuggles even though the nights are long.
Watch them go to preschool with their little backpack
on because soon it will be high school.
Show up to their games while they still want to play sports.
Read the books because they're still asking for you to do so.

It's going faster than we can keep up with,
you will not get these exact moments again.

Time isn't stopping, but you have the choice everyday
NOW to take a moment and really take it in.

You are your own journey and can change direction as you see fit.

Change your mindset.
Change your body.
Change your location.

Change what needs to be changed so you are waking up every day learning how to be on the best journey you can be.

What's one thing you can do this week to change your direction?! Maybe you need to commit to going for a walk, or drinking more water, or listening to a podcast.

I'm in a very specific mindset right now and I am willing to do anything to level myself up.

This week, I committed to reading more.
And it can be that simple!!

You get to choose every day.
And no matter what, keep going. •

Some serious journey love.

And one day you'll embrace your inner beauty.
And one day you'll rediscover your light.

And one day you will finally realize how amazing you are.
Just you.
Being you.
Finding all those little things you've hidden about yourself for so long.

It's time.
It's time to step out from the shadows you're hiding in
because we need to you show up just as you are.

The light that you have in your heart is only yours, and
was given to you to show the world, don't dim it.

I cut your leather, by hand.
Sometimes my kids will come down and help.
Strip by strip. Today a little hand wanted to help - well he wanted
to actually do it but I take my leather seriously so I let him 'help'.

I wanted you to know that I cut your leather with love every day.
No machine does it for me. And some days, you're lucky enough
to have little hands helping. They're as much of this company
as I am - and often are with me when your pieces are made.

I work from my home, with my family, and even though
there are many hard days that surround my business model,
there are days where I wouldn't have it any other way.

Showing my kids the power of hard work.
The choice to give back.
The reminder to show up every day.

Sending love to anyone who needs it.

As you conquer the mountains in front of you, I want you to remember to conquer the mountains inside of you too.

Part 15 of the Tutu Chronicles:

Those mountains that have been placed in front of you, are there because you are strong enough to conquer them. You know, the ones you talk about, the ones people may even help you climb. Those milestones you will get to the top of, only to see another one in the distance - one you will also succeed in conquering.

But not often enough do we talk about the unseen mountains. The ones that are inside of you, that no one else sees.

The anxiety. The self-doubt. The self-hate. The list goes on and on. All those internal things we forget we also need to conquer - imagine what we could do if we took steps to climb over both?

Imagine how beautiful and freeing it would be to learn how to love any mountain you find yourself in front of. Knowing you are strong enough to get over it.

Get out of your own dang way.
Learn how to say no thank you, I am ready for the climb and I will get to the top of whatever it is that's holding me back.
Internally and in your daily external life.

We can do it.
We are strong enough.
You just need a little extra push.

Just like I do.

PS. I packed around my tutu for this pic, and asked a random stranger to take pictures of me whipped it out of my purse and ran with it. I found it interesting after I looked at them, that an Inukshuk made it into the picture too.

This is what they stand for: Traditionally, they were used by the Inuit in the north as directional markers. An Inukshuk in the shape of a person signifies safety, hope and friendship.... Inuksuit have been transformed into a symbol of hope and friendship that transcends borders to reach people all over the world.

A marker. True direction. Up and over those mountains in front of you, with safety, hope and friendship pushing you over the top.

Love you friends

There is so much we need to remember when
it comes to the days we live.

Allowing ourselves to just be, wherever we are at in our
lives, is a grace that is learned - then appreciated.

Be comfortable where you are.
Be small then shout from the roof tops.
Stand tall, then take seat and observe.

Today. Be them all.
Then do it all again tomorrow.

Be love for yourself today.

*

Take a deep breath.
Let go of what you can't control.
Be grateful for the breath you just took.

Take a second to remember how lucky we are
to see the sunrise every morning.
It's really something I am thankful for every. Single. Day.

Now go out and do the best you can today, in whatever you're doing.
Even if you're going nap, make it the best dang nap you've ever had.

You are strong enough to carry this dream and you are strong enough to hold on to it when it takes longer or looks different than you imagined.

> Whatever your dream may be.
> You are strong enough.
> You carry it in your heart.
> So hold on.

> No road is ever straight.
> You'll get there.

No great adventure or story never had a steep hill or a twist in the road.
Yours won't either.
But there's beauty in the plan that's not planned.

Love where you are.
As you are.

I found this one in my closet and it was meant to be found. It was my favorite wrap last year and it's such a good and simple reminder.

We all have bad days, bad moments, things we wish we
could change or days that just don't seem to end.
Life, it's hard and can be so challenging and
beautiful all in the same day.

This is your reminder.
To accept what is going on, make changes if necessary,
but to never forget to love. where. you. are.
Today.
Not a year from now.
Not a month from now.
Right now.

Because right now is who you are, and there are
so many beautiful things about that.

Whatever you are doing today,
wherever you are,
even in your in between,
you got this!

I love Monday's now. They're my day to get organized, get back on track after the weekend and make some beautiful days with what the week brings me. Even if it brings the unexpected or the hard, you have to keep getting back up and pushing forward.

*

"you were encoded with irreplaceable genius,
born from unrepeatable chemistry"

Not one of us is the same.
Not one of us will have the exact same dream.
So find yours and show it to the world.
We need what you have hidden inside.

Of all the other beautiful things you will do
today, be sunshine for someone else.

Smile even if they don't smile back.
Hold door even if they don't say thank you.
Give a compliment even if you don't know them.

Because it's not about what they don't do, it's about
what you do, and what life you live.

I do these things all the time. They make me feel good, make me
thankful for little things in my life. It makes my life full and happy.

So go out today and be sunshine.
As if you weren't already.

Love bright today.

Do you know someone who is sunshine in human form?
Let them know today. Maybe they need a lift today.

You're never too old to believe in Christmas magic.

Part 16 of the Tutu Chronicles:

December.
The month of childlike wonder.
I still have that little girl inside who gets excited for all of the festivities, Christmas lights, movies, traditions, stockings etc.

Except now, I get to make it magical for my kids. It's my top priority this month. To make it so extra special they will always remember the little things we do together.

I'm that mom.
The mom who does the elf.
The mom who goes overboard on stuffing the stockings.
The mom who wants her kids to feel and believe in the joy, magic and wonder of Christmas for as long as they can.
Also I will still make them do these things as grown-ups. Or try anyhow.

Christmas magic is joy.

I wish we could bottle up parts of December and have that 'feeling' once a month for the entire year. There's just something about it.

Make this December magical.
For you. For your kids. For your friends.
However you can do it. Do it.

It's needed more than ever.

EMBRACE:
Invite and embrace happy moments.
Move with the flow of life, let the good come, and the bad go.

BALANCE:
Life is about balance.
The good, the bad.
The highs the lows.
The valleys and the peaks.
A reminder to let your light shine in the middle of it all.
You are your centre, you choose which way to go.

Let's start the day off right, with a reminder that you are YOU.

You have gifts that are YOURS.
You have a face that is YOURS.
You have a life that is YOURS.

So shine YOUR light.
Celebrate YOUR light.
And together, we will light up our towns, our
Country and this beautiful world.

Now get out there and be YOURSELF.

Daily dose of inspiration coming at you from - oh just me, Kim.
I get it. Some weeks are long, kids are a lot, laundry
is a lot, work is a lot, and we get so busy.
Too busy to remember what is beautiful about just being alive.
We woke up today.
We have a roof today.
We got to go outside and take a big deep breath of fresh air.

Start turning your mindset into finding the good in every day.
I know I say it a lot, but it's because I truly mean it,
and I truly live by it.

So my CHALLENGE for you today, is to
find one thing that is beautiful.
Just one. Find the joy in being alive today.

It's time.
It's time to take that one step you need to take and to stop playing small.
No matter what that means for you.

Do what you dream of now, so you won't regret never trying what has been placed on your heart. You already have it in you. That little spark of creativity or genius, you know it's there.

It's not even just yourself that you need to show up for. It's all the people who need what you have to put out in this world.

They don't even know they need it yet, because its there, sitting inside you, waiting to be shown, waiting to be put out there in some big way.

Lots of the podcasts I listen to ask, "who are you showing up for?" "who needs you to succeed?" I always say my family, my kids. I show up for them daily. But I had never said myself. I need to show up for myself too, for the people that need what I have to say or create.

So show up for yourself now so the future you that is waiting can celebrate when you get to her.

Love your future self.

This is your Monday morning,
two weeks left of this year reminder - to go and do something fun.

Part 17 of the Tutu Chronicles:

Found this gem looking for some pictures to print off.

I remember it like yesterday. Declan asked me to come scooter with him. He was showing me how to do all these tricks...we were just there, together, laughing and having the best time.

I was too scared to try anything he could do because one, I didn't want to break my face, two, I didn't want to break my shins and three, I was too scared of falling.

But I had one trick up my sleeve.
This was it.
And he was unimpressed but supportive

The best part?
We were together.
HAVING FUN.
I always want to be a part of my kids' lives and will do things when they ask. Even if it means risking my life on a scooter.

So this was my reminder that as we go into holiday mode, I will be getting up and doing MORE with them. Just to be with them.

Why? Because they want me too.
And one day they won't ask me like they do now.

So go have fun.
Do it for you. Do it for them.
Just do it.

There is Something Beautiful in Every Day

As you turn off the light switch, be thankful you have electricity.
As you wash your face with warm water, take a second and really feel
the warmth, be thankful you can wash your face with warm water.

As you lay your head down on your pillow, really feel the pillow.
Really feel the blankets that you are so lucky to be able to pull up
over you as you drift off to sleep. Knowing you are safe and warm.

Sometimes we forget these little things we naturally just do every day.

But actually these are huge things.

They make up our entire days, electricity, warmth, water...
and these are things I am thankful for every. Single. Day.

When we say what we are thankful for with the kids at
night we always end up giving thanks for our car and
the roof over our head, things like that. Every day.

It's important.

People want to do good.
They have it in their heart to do good
They just need to know how to do it
They don't know where to take donations so
I tell them to come and see me
As a group and a community we can change lives

We can change our community.
We can change someone's life.
We can show people that LOVE is out there
and it will end up taking over.

We need it to take over.

Whatever it might be.
It's in you.
You're here for a purpose.
All of us and the world need you and whatever it is you have.
So go.
Go and use it to change something.

I am here for it!
I am here for you!
Cheering you on and watching that little light shine.

Shine bright.

You get to drop your kids off at a safe school.
You get to drive in your car to work, that
allows you to put food on your table.

I get caught up in the, ugh, I have to do this and I have to do that.
And I know you do too. We all do. Right?

I really have tried hard to change the way I look at my day.

I get to make beautiful things.
I get to inspire others even though some days
I feel like I am so overwhelmed.
I get to wake up early and see the sunrise every morning.

Please take this with you into your day and
notice what you GET to do today.

Then go inspire others around you to do the same.

My logo.
It's not just a logo.
It's a way of life.
It's my way of life.
It's the way I want you to go into your life, moment by moment.

It's a reminder every day
To love more,
Be kinder,
And choose to truly live your life in a way that makes your heart happy.

Then on the days that are hard or sad to remind yourself
that there is something beautiful in every day.

This is what I see when I look at my watch, or my hat
or anything that this little gold heart is on.

But it's also what I want you to see.
It's also what I want you to remember.

It's not just a logo.
It's a reminder.

So go.
Live with as much brightness as this little gold heart.

I know I am.

Inspiration to JUST START

Do you have an idea in your heart?
Something you want to start but feel like you can't?

It doesn't even have to be a business idea. Maybe it's just hobby, maybe it's doing something for yourself - learning yoga, or taking a dance class.

I started with hardly anything and worked myself up to a $2,500 visa on which I ran my company for 5yrs.

You don't need huge amounts of money you just need to show up and figure out how to do what you need to do.

You need to be determined.
You need to be committed.
You need to be consistent.
You need to be rooted in your love for what you want to do.
You need to start.

I'm here for you.

Choose one that you need to hear right now:

1. Make the *time*.

2. Good things take *time*.

3. Take *time* to make your soul happy.

4. Give yourself *time*.

5. Don't wait. The *time* will never be just right

6. The greatest gift you can give someone is your *time*

7. No better *time* than now.

8. The best *time* for new beginnings is now.

9. It's *time* to run after the dream in your heart.

10. Trust the *timing* of your life.

Ps. Don't forget to have a good *time*.

Whatever you choose,
write it down, and live it.

This week was one of those weeks where I felt like I had 153 tabs open, needed to make some big decisions, needed to focus on one or two things at a time but was being pulled in 16 different places.

Some days it's hard to be the only one
responsible for making the choices.

Some days it's hard making financial decisions
that could end up being a disaster.

Some days I wish I had a boss and could just go home at the end of the day and forget until 9am the next morning when I got back to the office.

No one carries that weight. Just me.
And it's been a lot lately.

Then out of the blue, someone says something that is uplifting, encouraging and reminds you of all the other things you're doing right.

So I felt like I needed to say that if you are thinking of someone, if you have something to say to them and haven't, just do it. Reach out.

Tell them you thought their shirt was beautiful today, that they are doing a good job, that something they said made you think differently.

Whatever it is, say it.
When we life someone else up, we all lift up each
other, because the circle keeps going.

And you just don't know how much they might need it.

Support each other.
Lift each other.
Love on each other.
Someone needs you today.

Women like you don't happen very often, don't forget how rare you are.

Wonder Woman.
(plural Wonder Women)
1. (by extension) A woman of extraordinary powers; a superwoman.

Wonder Woman is a compassionate caring, stubborn, opinionated, highly competitive, outgoing, immortal Amazon.

Wonder Woman is warrior born.

Wonder Woman is fearless and focused on her objectives.

Doing extraordinary things in her regular daily life.
This is what it's about.
Showing up every day.
Supporting each other every day.

So much love to all my women out there.

Reminders for your week ahead.

We don't know what this week holds, or what it will throw your way, but you can set yourself up to be able to handle it all.

Just remember what's important.
Remember who you are.
Remember what your heart knows.

Remember what your heart knows.

Go get whatever you're after.

Be love this week.

♥

Small steps are progress
You are appreciated
Saying no is okay
Stop comparing
You are capable of amazing things
You are enough

Oh and that shirt looks great on you

♥

Momma's looks, Momma's eyes
Her old man's fightin' side
Stubborn heart, gypsy soul
Tell me where does the time go

Gonna dance with my daughter
Spin her around under the lights
'Cause I'm just a mother
Making the most of this moment in time
Before she lets me go, I'll hold her close
Caught in this race against time
Right now all I want is to dance with my daughter tonight

This song came on yesterday and that first
paragraph stopped me in my tracks.
So I picked her up and danced.

Today she is 10.
I'm not sure where the time has gone.
But I am sure that from this birthday on, we will dance. Every year.

To my sweet, kind hearted, animal adorer, rainbow
loving girl, you are my first baby, my life changer and I
can't wait to see what you will do in this world.

Happy Birthday Memphis.
Thank you for teaching me more about life than I ever thought possible.

Just LOVE.

No matter what.

Everywhere you look right now is a bit chaotic and the unknown of everything is a lot to try and make sense of.

Who do we believe, what is true...

What I know is that no matter what,
we are love.

We can still put love out there when others may be doing the opposite.

We can show up, love where and when we can, and prove that no matter what, that part of us that was built in before we were born, can stand any storm of unknown.

What is my heart.

Who am I, like really who am I.
I go back to the picture of the little girl dancing in the rain that says,
"remember her?" go find her!

Maybe in all this crazy, and time off, we can spend some
time being less busy, focusing on what matters,
which includes getting back to you.

Who you are outside of work, being a mom, being a wife or whatever.
Just you.

I don't know how or what that looks like, but maybe it starts
with picking up the book you've wanted to read. Or stepping
on the treadmill for the run you said you'd start.

Let's use this as a mini reset.
Maybe that will be the blessing in it all.

Now go find that part of you that you've put aside.

Just love.
The world needs more of it

We don't know what to expect right now.
But there's one thing I KNOW.

We have the choice to think positive.
We have the choice to help others.
We have the choice to take this time to pour
into our families and friends,
And check some things off the to do list.

But most of all we have the choice to love.

Snuggle in tonight.
Hold your kids hands.
Have a piece of chocolate.
Dream of summer.

Use this time.

However you want too.

Dance in the living room with your kids then turn
around and read that book you've been putting off.

Make your favorite salad, then make your favorite brownies.

Go for a long walk, take a nap.
It's in living,
We find our way back to ourselves.

Be love today.

♥

Because today, I curled my hair.
Because today, I felt good – mentally.
Because today, the sun was shining.
Because today, I looked at the wrinkles under
my eyes and saw life and laughter.
Because today, we went for a walk and felt the sunshine.
Because today, I sat in the sun as it was coming through
the window of my living room and had a coffee.

Because today, was a good day.
And the little moments showed me so.

Light the path.
Speak love and hope.
Call them to rise.
Show them their worth.
Write my story.
Empower them to write theirs.
Be beautiful.
Shine bright.
Be true.
Serve.

From me to you.

For you.

I see you.
All you wildflowers out there.

I see what's coming for you.
All the beautiful colors you will show off.

Every one of you different from the one beside you.
Growing in a new way.
In a stronger way.

Even if you feel buried right now,
remember all seeds must break through dirt first
to be able to show their true beauty.

Bella Vita.
English – beautiful life
Italiain – bella vita
Spanish – hermosa vida
Swahili – Maisha mazuri
Filipino – magandang buhay
Dutch – mooi leven
Icelandic – fallegit lif

Doesn't matter who says it, it means the same.

You woke up today?
Beautiful life.
You have running water?
Beautiful life.
You can make a grocery store run once a week?
Beautiful life.
You can feel the sun on your face?
Beautiful life.
Don't forget it.
Please, don't forget your life is so beautiful.

Today seemed extra hard in the self-love department.
It's hard because even I've said,

It's okay to not be okay.
Some days are unchartered waters.
No one knows how to feel sometimes.

But geez.
Some days, the not okay is just harder to get over.

All I know is that tomorrow is new.
Today I am grateful for so many things, like always,
But that doesn't mean I can't have a moment.

Sometimes you just need to walk, drive, have the treat, have a cry, have a bath, whatever you need to do to stay sane.

Do it.
Your kids need you.

But in order for you to be the best you,
You need to know when to take a second.
Or 10. Or half a day.
This is your reminder to go.
To your room.
Down a backroad.
To put on your headphones and sing.
Grab a chair and sit in the sun if you can –
and let those kids play on their iPad for and extra hour.

Do what works for you.

From one mama to another.
You got this.

All the tulips on my table were opening perfecting round.
Except one.

I didn't notice the perfect ones, I noticed this one.
I noticed the way it was opened so beautifully and free.

It was a reminder that you don't have to bloom
like the others to be beautiful.

You get to grow and open at your own pace,
the less perfectly round the better.

Beautiful, just as you are.

Who's to say you can't drive a jacked up old truck
and wear a sundress at the same time.

Who's to say you can't have tattoos and have a heart full of grace.

Who's to say you can't run a successful company
and be a mom at the same time.

Who's to say your wrinkles don't belong by your eyes,
they are part of your story.

Who's to say your life can't be messy and beautiful at the same time.

Who's to say you can't wear a bright red lip and sit on the
back of a tail gate on a backroad.

Who's to say you aren't allowed to feel
overwhelmed even at the tiniest things.

Who's to say you can't feel totally done with your kids and
love them with your entire heart, all at the same time.

That's right.
No one.
No one gets to say.
Because it's your life.

If you want to drive a jacked up truck, be a girly girl in your polka dot dress, shoot some guns, drink beer by a fire, do your makeup to go do nothing at all, then you go ahead and freakin' do all the things!!

You don't need permission to be who you are in your own heart.

Take that this week and run with it.

Just wanted to say hi, and make sure you are okay.
And tell you that you are doing a good job.
I just wanted you to know.

Because if I were to see you in person, I'd say the same thing.

How are you?
Actually.

And tell you no matter what that you're doing a
good job. Even if you feel like you're not.

You are.

And then I'd say,

Love you friend.

Just like I would in person.

But actually, this week:

Take a break if needed.
Go for a walk if needed.
Stop school it needed.
Close the laptop if needed.
Give the kids extra screen time if needed.
Hug said kids.
Always needed.

♥

When self-doubt enters your mind,
remember how far you've come.
Remember who the heck you are,
and go do the damn thing!!

Part 18 of the Tutu Chronicles:

Self-doubt. A real joy stealer.

I'm so guilty of allowing it to take over.
This collection launch
This photo shoot
Work - can I even do this?
Parenting

See self-doubt takes more than it gives.
And I'm a giver. Why do I allow it to take
so much of my mental space up?
It takes away from me being able to give at my fullest ability.

I'm trying to learn to free myself from the limits it puts on me.
Because you know what?
The launch - was successful!
The photo - turned out!!
Work - I'm doing the damn thing!
My kids - they're amazing!

The thing is, every day will knock you down in some
way, we don't need to be doing it ourselves.

Thank you thank you for your support today.
I am doing this dance (in my joggers not
the tutu today) for all your love.

I can't wait to make you all the things and give you little
pieces of joy to remind you you are worthy and loved.

How many of you have doubted yourself, wasted all that
precious time, and it ended up turning out great?

I see you.
Let's do this together and show it the way out the door.

Still in my basement.
Still raising money to feed the kids and those who need my help.
Still making quality pieces.
Still proving you can run a company, be a
mom, try your best and give back.

New total $40k+ raised.

New dreams.
New goals.
New reasons to keep going.

What's stopping you?

I'm here for you and the things you think you can't do.
Because you can.

You see a dirty coffee mug, but I see an afternoon coffee that was soul saving, and a much needed break.

You may see a kid who most likely has had a bit more time on the iPad than normal, but I see a boy who also needed a break.

My other kid to the left, making clay animals and watching tiktok because that's just what she wanted to do.

The dog is on the couch with me, actually sleeping on unfolded laundry, but he's comfy and also taking a break.

I'm here, watching them all, making sure they're ok, loved and safe. The house is quiet, and we all just needed a second.

Maybe today you checked all the things off your list.

Maybe today you let the kids do whatever they needed to so you could do whatever you needed.

I see you.

And I HIGH FIVE whatever dang decision you made so you could get through your day.

Make the Time.

Give yourself time.

Trust the timing of your life.

Have a good time.

Take time to make your soul happy.

Don't wait, the Time will never be just right.

It's time to run after that dream.

The greatest gift you can give is your time.

Sending you love this week.
And some encouragement.

You have whatever is thrown at you.
You are stronger than you think.
Your kids will be ok for an hour longer on
screen time if you need a second.
Order in if you don't have the capacity to cook. Or clean.
Leave the school work if you just can't do it.
Take the extra time to snuggle, the dishes can wait.
Take a nap.
Go have a coffee with your friend.
Sit in the sun, close your eyes and take a breath.

You are needed and you need to do whatever it takes
to keep yourself in a good state.

Mother's Day
As you most likely go about your day doing most of the same things you to every day, I want you to remember that on the days you feel like you can't make it to dinner, you are doing an amazing job.

You are loved and appreciated, and given these
kids because you are who they need.
To all the mamas out there.
Mamas who's kids are grown up and gone.
Mamas who have a baby in heaven.
Mamas who are just getting started.
We are all in this together.

Mama you are doing a great job
Even if you had to hide in the closet to eat
your chocolate so the kids don't see
It's called survival
You got this

You do what you need to do.
Put the kids outside on the porch.
Hide in the bathroom.
Sit in the car and crank the music.
Hide in the closet.

Take a second for yourself today,
No one will judge how you take that second

Sending all the mama love.

Love where you are.
Easier said than done some days.
Am I right?

I have reached for this cuff 100s of times over the last year. It's my go to.

Because there have been lots of times I didn't love where I was.
Whatever was going on that day, it wasn't where I wanted
my mind to be, or my heart to be. Or whatever it was.

It's been the simplest reminder for me.

To choose good on the bad days.
To love where I am - when I just don't.
To remember what's important.

To remember my heart.
Before it let the world tell me what kind of day I was going to have.

It's seen bad days.
It's seen bad weeks.
It's seen everything.

It's like it's a part of me.
It fits my wrist perfectly because it's been worn in.

It may sound silly to some. But for me, it's like
it's a mini security blanket some days.

Breathe in, breathe out.
You have whatever is thrown your way.
You are stronger than you know.
You are braver than you seem.
Take that little light shining inside of you and show up today.
If you need a bit of courage, here it is
for whoever needs to hear it.

Here's your little piece of courage.
Your little handful of brave.
With a pinch of love.

Hoping your day is good today.

I know for a fact I will never take for granted, the
luxury of living in a place with so much space.

With open skies, mountains and rivers.
Where only handful of people are.
Where nature slowly grasps at your heart
and says, just breathe and let go.
Where the kids can fish, find things to do, and be free.
Fresh air is the best medicine.
Being by the water is soul saving.

No fish today, but maybe they were staying in, away from
the hustle and bustle of the river like we were with life.

That's what I like to think anyhow.

Take the pictures.
And this isn't even a reminder for YOU to take them.
This is a reminder to your friends, your spouse, anyone who is around you that thinks, oh this would be a cute pic - grab your phone take the picture - of life, just happening. Then send it to them.

This weekend we looked for rocks a few times.
One of oasur fav things to do.
But a friend took a picture without us knowing and sent a few.
I only have these memories in my mind.
But now I have a moment captured in time so I can see how little he was 'that one May Long camping trip' or show him years from now, this is what we loved doing.

Last summer I was at the river and a mama was cuddling her baby (I was sitting behind her) and it was so sweet, the babies arm was so small, her other kiddos were playing and I just took a picture of it, got the courage to go up to her and say hey, send me your number, I want you to have this.
She was SO thankful.

It's a moment in time you don't even know you need the memory of.
So grab your phone, because we all know you have it, and give a friend the best gift - a picture of a time where life was just happening.
They'll have that forever.

We can get so caught up in what's going on that's wrong,
we can lose sight of what's actually going right.

You know that I want you to find something beautiful in every day.

I was going back in my pictures and found this one.
I sometimes feel like I was born in the wrong generation.
My heart feels happy in polka dots, in my '78 bronco, windows down -
like I could pull up to a tailgate party at an old drive in and do the twist

So I will share with you:

1. I loved the day this picture was taken. I was on the
tailgate of my truck on a dirt road in the sun.
2. This weekend, disconnecting and finding some peace
in my heart and mind in the middle of nowhere.
3. Today, both kids coming to hug me without
me asking. I held on longer than normal.

I always find many things about even a crappy day that are
beautiful but for me, these three came to mind first.

A little louder for those in the back.

You don't get to judge anyone on their choice.
Not now especially.
But not ever.

You don't know what someone is going through
or what their kids are going through.

Please be kind.
Please be understanding.
We need more love right now, not more comments
that make people feel less than.
Got it?
Ok good.

Be on with your day and remember this.
You get to choose your words.
So please choose wisely.

You can be both.

You can be happy and sad at the same time.

You can be adventurous and love routine too.

You can look strong and feel weak.

The best part is,
All of these make you who you are.

So let yourself be.
Whatever that is for you this minute, the next hour, tomorrow.

When you're Canadian, after the long cold
months +4 could basically be +30.

Part 19 of the Tutu Chronicles:

Almost warm enough for flip flops, but will most likely snow this week
so have to keep the gloves and boots ready, but sunroofs and windows
open because the air doesn't hurt your face and that sun is life giving...

Its International Women's Day - so here's a glass raise
to all you Women out there doing your thing.

Lifting others up, while learning to lift yourself up. Doing
the dang thing every day, whatever that means for you.

I see you, I am you.
Together we can make a difference.

Even if it's a tutu, a piece of jewelry or a
conversation, you can make a difference.

Yesterday felt like our first spring.
There will be another small winter, fake spring,
almost spring then hopefully just spring.

Soon there will be dead lawn. Can't wait!
Then green lawn.
Lawn chairs.
Driveway drinks.
Dry roads.
Fires.
Camping.
I can't wait for it all.

Oh and someone send the sun so I can change
the color of my legs. Like actually.

I see you ladies out there killing it.
Keep it up. I'll be cheering you on.
Even from my lawn chair.

"I know when I am having a tough day I
can put on one of your bracelets,
as a reminder to myself of all the great things in this world, and that
the tough days just make the good days that much greater. Your
work helps me take a step back when I really need it. To appreciate
all the people and wonderful things I have in my life already."

My why.
It's always been about what I can make for you so you
can have reminders to live your best days.

To remind you what's important and how blessed you
are to have opened your eyes this morning.
To know hard days will pass and it's what you do in those
hard times that make you stronger for the next day.

Love you friends.
You're my why.

Gracefully broken.
Beautifully standing.
Yes you are.
Beautifully standing.
Even if it doesn't feel like it.
You are.

I LOVE our little army of gold heart wearing ladies.
We are like a small gang of walking reminders for ourselves and others.
It makes me sit for a second and be so thankful for those
of you who believe in what I say and create.

It's me reminding you to find something beautiful in
everyday, you making that reminder a part of your life.
It's you choosing to see the joy and love in each
day, even if it's something little.
I LOVE being part of that kind of gang.

To my gold heart wearing army.
I am so thankful for you and this life we are going through together.

Because one day he will be taller than me.
Because one day he will be older and maybe not
so willing to wrap his arms around me.

Because I can smell the top of his head.

Because the way he looks up and puts up his arms for me
to pick him up, jumping and wrapping his legs around me.
Even now, that moment is getting harder to come by.
Because there's only so many more times
I'll be strong enough to lift him.
There's a lot going on in everyone's days right now. So many things.

Take a break from what's making your heart feel crazy and
remember the little things that make your heart feel whole.

Sending love today to:
everywhere and anywhere

everyone and anyone

*

Anything is possible with a brave heart.

Friend,
Your heart is brave.
Brave for whatever you're going through.
Brave for what you need to do.
Brave because it's yours.

That makes anything possible.

Find the things and the people that make you feel like your best self.

The things that make you feel whole.

Fill yourself up with them.
For when you are lost and struggling to find your way...

These are the people, places and things that will
help you remember who you are again.

That help you remember who you are again.

*

Let yourself become...
Yourself
Strong
Beautiful
New
Peaceful
Loved

Whatever it is, let yourself become...and
unbecome everything you aren't

Because no matter what, this is your ONE beautiful, beautiful life..
Even if some days it doesn't feel like it,
It's yours and its beautiful.

And it's our only one.

*

There you are
My friend with the beautiful smile.
Yes that one.
That smile will change the world so make sure you use it every day.
Yes that smile.
It's yours and yours only.

Given to you, the only one of its kind, to change the world with.

Show up with it every day.

It looks beautiful on you.

Sky.
Hearts.
Two of my favorite things.

Dark clouds, but not dark enough to stop light.
Hard weeks, but not hard enough to stop me.

Don't ever let the dark stop your light.
Your light is what this world needs.

When you're finding yourself.
When you're listening to yourself.
When you're doing things that make you feel peaceful.
When you are letting go of things that are holding you back.
When you make mistakes and learn from them.
When you remember who you are and what your heart wants.

Heart happy.

Whatever that means for you.

It's your reminder, to do the things that make your heart happy.

Because sometimes simplicity makes me happy,
and the reminder is all I need.

Stripped down, nothing colorful surrounding it,
just myself and the middle of nowhere.

I am learning to be heart happy.

You know I love old things.
I love stories.

Buttercup the bronco
Born in '78.
I've always wondered, WHO was the one to walk into that
Ford dealership and say "that one, she's the one I want.
Drive her off the lot and give her a home.

Was it their first new truck?
How long did they save for to get her?
The back seat.
Who's been back there? Kids? Friends?? Okkkk,
and yes probably that too it was the 70s
Her roll down windows.
Her dusty seats and dash.
Which I don't clean on purpose.
The way she smells, like my dad's old fencing trucks.
Sometimes I drive barefoot just because it feels like I should.

She carries so many stories and I plan on keeping
that book going for a long time.

Find a piece of your soul this week.
And when I say that, I mean a piece that you've set aside
Find it.
Pick it up.
Put it back in your heart.
Don't let it go.

Let's find all the little pieces of ourselves that we've put aside.

It's your week.
You got this.

Every summer has a story.

Every year we write a different chapter in our summer stories.

This year might be the biggest chapter yet,
depending on how you look at it.

So make it yours.

Make it interesting, fun, different and full of life.
Because summer is just one chapter of many, and it's yours to write.

This isn't a picture to show off my cute necklace.
This isn't a picture to show off my super cute red heels
which I may never wear as they make me 6'3" tall.

This is a picture of a girl wearing a white t-shirt. A white
t-shirt that she's never felt she could wear. That she's
never felt confident in, and still doesn't really.

But her desire to let go of the issues she has with her body is
starting to outweigh not wearing what she wants to wear.

I know you have that one outfit that you can't wait to wear one day.
If you could just lose the 5lbs or find the right pair of jeans.

But sista, I am here to encourage you to find that confidence,
to know you are beautiful at the size you are right now.
To let go of what you 'think you should' look like in your dream
outfit and make that outfit look beautiful because it's you in it.

I used to weigh 255lbs and have struggled ever since to feel
comfortable in this new strong and different body. I'm tired of
feeling this way, and am going to make sure I just go live my life.

One white t-shirt at a time.

Because I tell you that there is always something beautiful in everyday, this was one of a few things that was beautiful in my day.

I left the mail, got into my car and the song that was playing was 'Leave her Wild' by Tyler Rich.

I looked over and these daisies were just dancing in the wind, being beautiful in their own wild. I sat and watched them, took a second and thought this is just a good moment. So I jumped out and hit record.

So I am sharing it with you.

Start noticing. Beauty is all around you.

And if you haven't listened to the song it's a must.

Here's part of it...

If you find a girl, hands up, hangin' halfway out on the highway,
You find a girl who likes whiskey mixed in her hangover coffee...

If you're gonna kiss her, if you're gonna kiss her kiss her slow
If you wanna change her, if you wanna change her Let her go
If you're gonna let her, if you're gonna let her
Let her dance, let her sing, let her be what ever she wanna be
If you're gonna love her, if you're gonna love her
Leave her wild
@tylerrich

What did you do today?
vs
What did you want to remember about today?

I love this perspective.

I love things that make me think differently about something that I've thought the same about for so long.

Because why the heck not.

Is there a perspective quote you love?

My other favorite one is...
Change your 'I have too' to 'I get too'

I get to wash the dishes. It means I had food to eat. I get to go to work. It means I can pay my bills and do fun things.

Sending love today everyone.

Too tall. Too short.
Too heavy. Too light.
Too sexy. Too modest.
Too wild. Too boring.
Too colourful. Too mundane.
Too country. Too city.
Too much. Too little.
Too careful. Too carefree.
Too happy. Too sad.
Too many tattoos. No tattoos.
Too strong. Too weak.
Too different. Too similar.

Too. Much. Dang. Noise.

My challenge for you is to let go of any contradicting thoughts that anyone including yourself may have been placed on you.

You are not too tall, too sexy, or too wild.

You are you.

You are _____.

Fill that in for yourself and put it in your pocket and walk with your head tall. Drop anything else that's holding you back.

I will go first:
I am tall. I am strong. I am colourful. I am different and I am learning to find my wild and my sexy.

Even if you don't share here, write it down for yourself at home. If you do want to share, I'm giving away a bracelet set to a random comment. This is important!

The only thing you aren't, are all the words placed on you that don't belong. So drop them off, and only pick up the ones of the girl you see looking back at you in the mirror.

♥

Remember.
That dream was planted in your heart for a reason.

Part 20 of the Tutu Chronicles:

Whatever it is.
When your heart is still saying - hey you, we should do this...I know it might be hard, I know you don't have it all figured out, I know you don't know how it will work out, but we need to try. We will figure it out. Or maybe we won't.

You should do the thing

I SOLD OUT of my first box in HOURS!! HOURS! You guys showed up and are so excited which makes me crazy happy.

SO...
What if it works out?
What if you succeed greater than you even thought.
What if it challenges you in a new way, and you find a new part of yourself you needed to meet?

And you're right. Not everything works out.
But it's better to try and let that 'could be' dream pass so the 'real dream' can come forward. That's how we learn. That's how we grow.

The Beautiful Love Boxes - I've been thinking of them for years. Logistically - too much to think about. Then how, what if and what if it doesn't work? Always setting it aside because it was too much. I finally decided it was time to see which way the 'what if' was going to go.

It was taking up so much space in my heart it either needed to be done and succeed or try and have it not work. Either way I had to try.

And you guys. You guys helped make my dream come true.

My heart kept pushing me. I just had to listen.

So thank you for always being here.
Thanks for helping me push myself.
I couldn't do it without you.

Step into it ladies.

I am learning to accept myself. Even the part
of me that can't accept myself.
So every time you open your phone,
you are reminded to accept your beautiful self as you are.
Not five pounds from now. Not when your skin gets better.

Right. Freakin'. Now.

It's a process. Learning to love those parts of us we struggle with.
But we can do it together.

You got this you gorgeous lady.

When I was in Charleston, Brendan Burchard
made me have an AHA moment.

He said, how many times have you accomplished something
and then right away moved onto the next thing?

Why don't we take time to sit back and say holy crap I did
that? I got to this goal and now I'm going to celebrate and take
a minute to allow myself to feel what was accomplished.

I never do that.
Sell out of hoodies? Omg I have to figure out how to get more.
Watch sell out? Crap! I need more. I need the next design.

I'm always onto the next thing I need to get done.

But with anything, you learn.

I just finished the largest order of my life in two weeks,
prepped for a show, got orders done. Did all the ordering,
hosted a show and completed it with a massive success.

First time ever I am allowing myself to sit for a second before I move on.

Fall/winter is my busiest season and I'm taking a
moment before I start all my thinking.

Please. Please learn to celebrate even the tiniest victories.

You ran today? Celebrate yourself.
You wore that dress today? Celebrate.
You completed that huge project at work? Cheers to you.

It's time to recognize what we've done and allow ourselves to feel it.

PS. I wore a full on white dress tonight.
White T-shirt? White dress? Who is this girl?
I'm not sure but she's staying.

Let go.
Forgive yourself for whatever it is you are carrying.

The weight of hate is far too much for any of us to bear.

Especially hate towards ourselves.

I'm sending out so much love to whoever needs it.

I am the first to tell you I carry more than I need too
for myself and it's something I am learning.

The world needs forgiving myself me.
Which means the world needs you forgiving you.

Because I want my kids to know that I work hard but I don't want them to remember me 'always' working.

Because I want my kids to know that even though I am busy, I will always make time for them.

Because I need to remember they will only hold my hand for so long, and there is no amount of busy that can take that away.

Because I am busy, and these past months have been long and crazy feeling and I felt 100% like every time they needed me or asked for me I wasn't there.

I felt like I hadn't 'seen' them.
Or 'felt' them.

This vacation has been so needed.
Declan has asked me for more hugs a day than ever. Just random hugs.
I'm holding his hand everywhere we go.
I mean really holding it.
Memphis has asked for more kisses than ever.

The reset was needed.
And I've promised myself going into my busy season that the second I feel like I am pushing my kids away for work that I will stop and go to them before anything else.

Because they're the most important thing I will build.

Because we are made up of so much more than numbers
on the scale,
or the stories we tell ourselves about what we are doing wrong.

We are made up of so many beautiful things we forget to count them.

Let's focus on the parts of us that make us beautiful to others,
so we can learn to focus on being beautiful to ourselves.

You are beautiful, just as you are.

Sometimes I just go to where my wraps are
and close my eyes and grab one.

Today this is what I grabbed.

What a reminder as I was fighting with
something right along these lines.

This cuff has been with me for about two years. It's worn, it
fits my wrist shape perfectly, it's seen good and bad days.

But the reminder stays the same.
It's been the same for 2yrs.
And I've needed it every now and then for the entire time. Daily really.

My everyday bracelets have been on my wrist
for almost as long! Just about 2yrs!
They don't come off so they've been with me on every battle and
amazing day since I put them on. They're almost ready to break
and I hate it when it happens. Like a release in a way but they've
been a part of me for so long I miss our little journeys together.

This is never just jewelry to me.
It's a part of me.
It's a part of my days and my own little
reminders for myself. No one else.

Today is the oldest you've ever been and the youngest you'll ever be again think about it.

You're working?
Get a special coffee.
At home with the kiddos?
Lock yourself in the bathroom with a wine.
Camping?
Sit outside and notice nature and take some good deep breaths.

Whatever it is, find a piece of joy in it.

Go live!

Sometimes I get to see how far I've come, and then sometimes it gives me the reminder I need.

You know since I started, this was never just about bracelets. It was about you, and making your life happy, inspired and giving you the little nudge you need to live your best one.

I get to be there through all the stories, chapters and times you need to pull yourselves up. But that's what a friend does.

It just so happens that I get to be the little cherry on top of those days for you, encouraging you along, one bracelet stack at a time.

So go change the world this week and every week after, because we can.

If I asked you to name all the things you love, how long would it take for you to name yourself

I have this quote on the wall I see first when I enter my workshop.

A constant reminder that I built this.
From nothing.

Through all the mistakes, HUGE mistakes, celebratory moments, mountains I had to climb...

From nothing, came something.

Head into this week, with the reminder that you can do what's on your heart.

You can choose to serve the world with the gift you have.

It won't be easy.

You'll work harder at this than anything in your entire life.

But if you have a calling, it's yours.
You need to go after it, one cry fest, almost punch a hole in the wall, shout from the roof tops, day at a time.

But you're strong enough to do it.
It wouldn't be yours if you weren't.

Now go build.
From nothing.
Into something.

I will always see the world for what it could be

I've always felt like I see things differently.
Like I feel things differently.

Like I can see what the world could be if we just did more.

I have always felt different, and it's not until having this community from my company that I found a place to show up.

Not only for myself but for the people in my community and my page.

My heart is always so full of hope and wonder
and I know some people aren't like that.
That's ok.

But it's who I am.
So I will show you how I see the world in hopes that it will rub off on you so you can see it in the same way.

Sending love where it's needed today.

You will fall more times than you thought possible.

But you will ALWAYS get back up.
More times than you thought possible.

This goes with everything in your life.
Your business. Work. Family. Kids. Spouse. Activities.
Yourself. Anything and everything.

Keep going.
And rise.

I know you can.

You were given something no one else has...YOU.

You are who you are,
because YOU are what the world needs.

SO stop trying to be someone else.

No one has the gifts you do.
The smile you do.
The laugh that you do.
The spark in your heart that you do.

You were put here for a reason, so show up in who
you are and let everyone else do the same.

I am always wanting to inspire you to live your best life.

Keeping the reminders we need close, so we can
show up every day in this beautiful life.

Crazy times call for crazy amounts of love
So go be crazy.

Love more than usual.
Be kinder than usual.

We can choose love everyday…
or you can choose the other thing.

But that way won't change the world.
Or the way you see it.

There's only one way.
So go crazy using it.
It will change the world and the way you see it.

One of my favorite things;
Curtains blowing in the breeze.
It is so relaxing to me.

Then there's the way the sun feels on my face.

The way fall smells.

The way the smell of fresh brewed coffee stops
me in my tracks and makes me smile.

It's always been about the little things.

Last year this time we were all planning on Thanksgiving celebrations without one care or worry. No pandemic in the plans.

This year so many won't be able to see their family members.

So for those of you WHO CAN...

Please.
Take it all in.
Kiss your mom.
Listen to ALL the stories.
Laugh at the dysfunction.
Even if you have to hold your eyelids open while Uncle Ted is telling the same story he does every year...

Be grateful for the normal.

Because even though it's different, if you're eating turkey, you have family and friends around your table, that normal is beautiful.

Maybe more beautiful than any other year.

So sit in it.
Be there.

Even if your Grandma is pinching your cheeks for the 100th time.

Let her.

BE HAPPY
BE HAPPY!
Because my sweater matches my Bronco - and I'm still driving her!
Thank you fall!!

Because my pink lipstick matches my favorite pink sports bra.

Because it's Friday.
AND a long weekend.

Because I worked my ass off all week.
Because you placed orders all week.

Because I saw my ladies for lunch today and it's
been a year since we've all been together.

Because my dog has the softest ears.

Because the sun was shining.

Because I WOKE UP today.

Because honestly I'm just a HAPPY person.

So Be Happy this weekend too.

I bet you can find ONE thing.
There's always one thing.

♥

It's a new week. Put down what was heavy about
last week, it's not yours to carry.

Things you can carry: how good you want to feel today.
How much love you can give, starting fresh with your thoughts,
finding one beautiful thing about your day, your own heart

Put down what's heavy.
Forgive yourself for whatever you need too.
Rest a little extra if you feel like it.

I honestly haven't felt myself the last couple days. I haven't
felt good in what I am wearing (for days) my mind has
been overwhelmed and full...you know how it is.

But tonight I'm clearing it out and starting fresh.

Because I'm not starting my week off thinking
about things I can't go back and change.

I will do better this week.
I will put down what doesn't need to take up space in my mind.
I will listen to the music and podcasts I love.

I will ALWAYS find something beautiful in every day.

I will carry my own heart through the ups and downs
of this week and start fresh again when needed.

Leave a heart if you will too.

♥

Because I'm learning to love myself.
While finding myself at the same time.

There's an odd peacefulness, a calm - like seeing an old
friend that you love so much but haven't seen in a while,
and like meeting a new friend at the same time.

But it's you and you.
Finally getting to know each other.

It's like I've gotten to an age where womanhood has
gently grabbed my hand and said, ok it's time.

It's time for you to let go of those little hang ups you have
about things you can't change. Because they don't matter.

It's like she's saying it's time for you to feel like the
person I've been waiting for you to be.

You have all these beautiful traits.
Yet you overlook them to see the things you don't like. Stop it.

You don't show up like you want to some days because
you're unsure of how it will make others feel. Stop it.

It's time to KNOW what and who is important,
and what and who to be free of.

It's time to show up as the woman you are. Anyone
who doesn't like it can step aside.

This change has come with age.
The last couple years I've been feeling different. But the last couple months I've let my mind catch up with my heart.

More friendship with myself and the life I'm living now, not just when I 'figure my shit out.'

Who else feels this or has found this.
Any advice you can give to those who might need it?

This is for all of you.
Because at some point she will grab all of our hands.

The ups and downs of owning your own company.
A constant tug o war between good days and
crappy days. Highs and lows.

Today was great and shitty all at once.

But it's another stepping stone of building my foundation.

To be stronger, do more and take myself higher
than I can even expect of myself.

Because friends we won't grow, change and find out about
ourselves if we don't go through the trenches.

So let yourself feel it.
But get up. Be resilient. Be consistent.
Build that mountain.
Then build a castle at the top.

New month.

May we start it with hope that good and
easy moments are on the horizon.

May we really learn to find joy in the smallest moments.

Because we get to choose.

We get to choose our own joy,
our own happiness and to love more even in the
uncertainty.

So choose to find all of the above, because
its' there, you just have to see it.

At least I'm a fun hot mess.

My house is lived in.

Sometimes I push the laundry off the bed
so I can go so sleep. The horror!!

My workshop is an actual hot mess.
My mind is usually a hot mess.

But.
My kids are happy. And here.
We run around like crazies, give the best hugs and laugh every day.

This beautiful hot mess of a life is ours and
I wouldn't have it any other way.

Do something FUN today.
The dishes can wait,
your soul usually can't.

Speak? Let me step into my HELL YES

Sometimes, the plan you have for your day, isn't your plan at all.

Second day of the life changing Rise Conference here
in Lake Louise. That I was attending to learn and
grow and be around like minded women.

Then something happened.
The beautiful Mandy asked me to get up and speak.
SAY what? To the what what? I was there as an attendee. Not a speaker.
But I couldn't say no, so I stepped into my
HELL YES and got on that stage.

The synchronicity of this weekend has been
unlike anything I've ever experienced.

I had written out the cards for the cuffs I donated over a month
ago. Each speaker spoke about remembering who you are -
unintentionally. Then I show up with cards saying the EXACT
same thing, cuffs reminding the women of the exact same thing.

Listen to those heart nudges. If I didn't I wouldn't
have made it here, wouldn't have been on stage and
wouldn't have made a new lane for my life.

Thank you for the opportunity to STAND IN MY COURAGE.

Geez.
Today. I still can't take it all in.

This weekend.
All about the nudges.
How through all the odds of getting here the nudges were strong.
Stronger than what my mind 'thought' I should do.

So my reminder for you.

I've said it before. That little spark you have in
your heart - it's yours. Yours only.

Follow it.
Follow the little push it gives you.

Start the side gig.
Sign up for the online conference.
Call that person.
Gift someone your gift.

I always gift people items when I feel like they need it.
Yes it takes time. Yes it costs me. But nothing is worth more to me
than seeing their faces when they get something unexpected.

The nudge to make, create and give has never lead me
anywhere but to where I feel more like myself than ever.

Heart nudges.
It's a thing.

Get out of your comfort zone and live for where they might take you.

I bet it's amazing.

When you buy from me,
you are buying a piece of my heart, a part of my life, a piece of my soul.

You are buying hours of mistakes, tears and happy dances.

Most importantly you are buying me more time
to keep going and follow my dream.

To donate back to my community, to purchase within my community.

To show my kids that their mama can work hard and make a difference.

To change the world one heart at a time

Can we talk about 'self- celebration' for a second?
I'm not even sure if that's a 'thing' but we are making it a thing.

I've wanted this jacket for over three years. Every time I
walked into Aritzia I would try it on and put it back.

I would think ok, todays the day. I'm doing it. It's coming home with
me...Ugh, no, I will leave it. I don't need it right now. I'll get it next time.

See, I have no problem spending money on
others, but find it hard to do for myself.

After I left Lake Louise, I had 7hrs until my
flight left so I ran into the mall.
For us Northern girls, this is a luxury we do not have.
A mall. With actual stores.

There it was. Aritzia. Always decorated so beautifully. I walked in and
this jacket was sticking out from the rack. In the most perfect color.

See. Just the day before I had gotten asked to be on stage
and speak. And I did it. I got my courage and did it.
I should celebrate that accomplishment.

Then after, the host asked me to be a Keynote Speaker at
the next conference. Um pardon? Yes. Yes I will absolutely
be there and speak some truth to some women.

I should celebrate being asked to be a keynote
speaker. That's a huge deal.

So. I grabbed the jacket. Put it on. Went back and forth. Maybe I should wait for Black Friday. Texted a friend. Said should I - shouldn't I?!

THEN. My heart was like you should celebrate this weekend. Not only for what happened. But for who you met. Who you became. What you learned. Moments you won't forget.

CELEBRATE you.
CELEBRATE accomplishments.
CELEBRATE life.

When a mother forgives herself, her heart takes a deep breath.
Hardest job in the world.

But you're doing it.
Even on the days you think you're not,
you are doing a great job.

You are only human.
Trying to raise tiny humans in a crazy time.

You're doing the best you can.

What's most important?
Those kids know they're loved.
That's it.

So drop the other expectations and know they think the world of you.

Just as you are.

Exhale.

Work hard.
Stay frickin consistent.
Persevere.
Make mistakes.
Learn from them.
Use them as the foundation of the company or life you're building.

You can do things you didn't think were even on your radar.

Like GQ. And Vanity Fair.

Like knowing and being with all of you every day.

Just so you know those two things are equal in value to me.

Keep going.

This is 38.

Learning about who I am.
Finding parts of me I lost.

Things I love:
Oversized tshirts.
Jogging pants.
Coffee.
Tattoos. I have 16. Maybe an addition this week
I am a romantic.
I love giving.
Old trucks.
Fast cars.
Old stories.
Country music.
I love anything that means anything.
Campfires.
Camping.
Side by siding.
Fishing.
Shooting guns.
Sunrises/sunsets.
Holding my kids hands.
Christmas.
Cedar boughs.
Life.

I love love.
I actually have love tattooed on me four different ways

Love on my palm, Japanese love (highschool lower back) and my kids writing of love from my birthday card last year on my ribs.

A little birthday story.
My Great Grandpa died December 7, 1937
My Great Grandma died December 7, 1967
My Great Aunt died December 7 not long after that.
These were my Grandpas parents and sister.

Then I was born December 7th.
Grandpa used to say I was the one who changed the meaning of this day.

7 has always been my favorite number. Even
before it had a meaning behind it.

I love stories and that's part of mine.

Thank you for being here with me on this journey of life.

I'm thankful for another year.

So go today, find someone to ask about part of their story,
and maybe in that you will find a part of yours.

I don't put random words on my clothes.
I put things that matter.
Words to live by.
Sayings that inspire.

Love more.
Be kind.
Stay true.

Because this entire world needs you to love more. It needs to be loved more.

Because this entire world needs you to be kind. And others to be kind back.

Because this entire world needs you to stay true to what is important to you. To stay in your lane, and stay true to your values.

I'm seeing it every day.
People knocking others choices.
People choosing harsh words thinking they might hold more weight than kind ones.

They don't.
Ever.

So in the crazy state that our world is in right now, maybe just maybe you can be the one that says something or does something inspiring.

So go be light today.
Because heaven knows our world needs it.

♥

All it takes is one rock to start a ripple.

If you focus on the positive you will see more positive.

If you focus on the negative you will see more negative.

So let's just erase that last sentence.
Read what's good.
Write down what's good.

Find something beautiful out of all the chaos and uncertainty.

We have two weeks left of 2020.

I'm not leaving this year mad or upset with what it's thrown at us.

I think we all realized what is important in each of our lives. We were forced to slow down and remember simple things I think we were rushing past in all our 'busy'

I've seen more giving and coming together for those that need it.

I've seen people remember that TIME with friends and family won't be taken for granted ever again.

Time. Together. With whoever that means for you. Let's not forget how it felt to not be able to see each other and make sure when we can that we really dive into conversations and be present.

"A ship is always safe at shore.
But that's not what it's built for."

Funny how things work.
The other day I was getting friend'ships' tattooed with some friends. I said there's a second meaning to this tattoo, one of my favorite sayings...

Then I got home to look for a cuff for a customer and this one with the exact quote was sitting right on my shelf. So naturally I scooped it for myself.

Because the truth is, we are always safe where we feel comfortable. And that's ok! That's such an amazing part of life.

But we are also built for growing, adventures and leaving the shore every once in a while.

To see new things, find pieces about ourselves we didn't even know...to show others how to shine their light and navigate their rough waters when needed.

All my orders are closed for Christmas but I want you to start thinking about quotes or words you're going to take with you into 2021.

I can't wait to see what we create together.
The reminders you will wear.
The quotes that will get you through.

For right now, this isn't leaving my wrist.

Because I'm going further than the shore I left in 2020.

Went for breakfast this morning.

I've posted about this before but today I feel like
it is something we need to remember.

Little cups of diner coffee.
Sugar and cream container bowls which leads to cream towers.
People sitting together.
Tired morning eyes.
Some unbrushed morning hair.
Music in the background but you can hardly hear it
because it's drowned out by all the conversations.
The tables are laughing.
People are together.

You know what it feels like?
It feels so normal.
Like nothing else is happening in the world.

We need more diner breakfast mornings.
Because they are raw and beautiful and classic.

I bet the grandpa beside us has been doing diner breakfasts for longer than I've been alive. At least I like to think so anyhow.

**I know some provinces can't go for breakfast and I also wish we could have our family and friends over like we can sitting at a restaurant table, but this is more about the moment I had this morning and hope that one day things will feel this normal again.

I am not beautiful like you.

I am beautiful like me.

I want to remind you of so many things this year. And I'm going to.

But the most important thing, the one thing I want you to drop before we even get to the new year, is comparing.

With everything.

You were given your heart, your talents, your beautiful smile, everything - right down to that weird pinky toe - I know you have one...

There is no one in the WORLD like you.
How amazing is that.

We are so quick to forget how amazing we are, as we are. I'm not saying you can't better yourself or take care of your looks - I'm saying do it for you...

Somehow you feel like you need to be like someone else in the world. Somehow you have been conditioned to not feel good enough as you are.

Drop this right now.
Drop the need to compare.
Drop the desire to look or be someone different.
Drop the excess stress you put on yourself every single day, because you feel like you can't show up as you.

I learned a lot about myself in 2020.
My confidence.
Really trying to find Kim again.
Remembering who I am.
Finding comfort in my own skin.

I did a good job. There's still a lot to be done.
But shit, it was just the beginning.

I'm going to help you break that shell you've
placed over your soul this year.

We are going to break each other open.

Starting with reminding you that you are beautiful
like you - because there is only one.

I hope in this book you have found inspiration.
Not each page will have been for you.

But I am hoping that the one page that was,
came on the day it was needed.

That you found a piece of yourself again.
That you picked up a little bit of brave and
courage when you needed it the most.

Because in writing for you,
I do the same.

I love you.

Kim

Posts from 2019/2020
Sand and Stone Jewelry
@sandandstonejewelry

CPSIA information can be obtained
at www.ICGtesting.com
Printed in the USA
BVHW060429281121
622636BV00003B/9